D0201557

Pastor Keyne

Friendship Evangelism

The Caring Way to Share Your Faith

ALSO BY ARTHUR G. MCPHEE . . .
Traveling Light

Friendship Evangelism

The Caring Way to Share Your Faith

Arthur G. McPhee

Foreword by Myron Augsburger

ZONDERVAN
PUBLISHING HOUSE
OF THE ZONDERVAN CORPORATION
GRAND RAPIDS, MICHIGAN 49506

FRIENDSHIP EVANGELISM
Copyright © 1978 by The Zondervan Corporation

Fifth printing 1981

Unless otherwise indicated, quotations from the Old Testament are from *The Revised Standard Version* copyright © 1946, 1952 by the Division of Christian Education of the National Council of Churches of Christ in the United States of America; and New Testament quotations are from the *New International Version*, copyright © 1973 by the New York Bible Society International.

Library of Congress Cataloging in Publication Data

McPhee, Arthur, 1945-
    Friendship evangelism.

    Bibliography: p.
    1.   Evangelistic work.   I.   Title.
BV3790.M27   269.2   78-17344
ISBN 0-310-37311-5

All rights reserved. No part of this publication may be reproduced, stored in a retrieval system, or transmitted in any form without the prior permission of the copyright owner, except for brief quotations in literary reviews.

Printed in the United States of America

To my wonderful wife, Evie

Contents

Preface

Foreword by Myron S. Augsburger

Acknowledgments

My gratitude to the following persons who contributed significantly to the making of this book: Lowell Hertzler and Paul Yoder, who encouraged me to write it; Evelyn Sauder, my typist; and Myron Augsburger for writing the foreword.

Preface

Both Christians and non-Christians are uptight about evangelism. One reason why is because of the unnatural, canned approaches that are so often recommended and used. Christians want to share their faith, but not as high-pressure salesmen. Non-Christians, on the other hand, have grown wary of religious "zealots" who are out to corner them and put them on the spot. Who can blame either group?

However, evangelism doesn't need to be conducted that way, and I doubt that it ever should be. The best evangelism takes place in a context of mutual trust and respect. It takes place between friends.

Friendship Evangelism: The Caring Way to Share Your Faith, seeks to show why your greatest witness is your deepest relationship, what such a relationship means in the overall task of making disciples, and how such a relationship comes to be. The book is not intended to be exhaustive, but introductory. It is hoped, however, that it will be freeing. Too many of God's potential witnesses are bound by fear and guilt. Too often the salt of the world is bottled up and the light of the world is blotted out because of discomfort with methods, not the message. Maybe the thoughts contained between these covers can help change that.

—Arthur McPhee

Foreword

Evangelism is God's extension of His grace through believers who engage in sharing the life of Christ with others. Too often evangelism is thought of as a function rather than a fellowship. In this very stimulating book, Art McPhee has done the church a special favor in outlining the priority and character of "friendship evangelism."

While the nature of our evangelism as a church will emerge from the nature of the evangelizing group, the style of evangelism must be adapted to the times and the culture in which Christians are sharing faith. Friendship evangelism is one of the more universally acceptable methods because it utilizes normal relationships. It has the potential of maximum participation of the membership of a congregation, and it offers a means of direct interchange with the public. And this sharing of faith is done in a context of loving acceptance of persons as individually important to us.

Theologically evangelism is based on God's purpose of building a kingdom of persons in fellowship with Himself. This is understood and experienced through Jesus Christ, in whom alone God is fully known and understood. In this sense, reconciliation is the central aspect of Christ's work and consequently should be seen as central in theology.

Evangelism is not an appendage to theology, or to the life of the church, but is an essential aspect of the divine purpose for man, i.e., reconciliation.

It should also be recognized that the church exists by evangelism. The church is a fellowship of redeemed sinners, in whose midst the living Christ is present by His Spirit. It comes into being as persons come to Christ. And each person who is a part of Christ's body has become a participant by a conscious response to God's call of grace. A truly New Testament church is always a first-generation church! Evangelism is thus the foundation of church development.

So long as evangelism is viewed as one function among others carried on by the institutional church, it will fail. So long as we fail to see its central place in a theology of reconciliation, we will not succeed in revitalizing the mission of the church. But with an awareness of the theology of evangelism as God's reconciling grace extended through us who believe, we can witness a revitalization of the church itself and a penetration of society with the Good News of grace.

Friendship evangelism, with its relational character, can function in a spirit of accepting love. In methods which speak to people at a distance, the element of love is less personal. In fact, one gets the impression that at times we "love people and hate persons." Friendship evangelism means participation in a relationship of love. And in a broken, alienated society, the ministry of love touches people at the point of their felt needs. As Michael Green said at the Lausanne Congress, "We must rediscover that the church itself is part of the kerygma." It is good news to announce to a lonely, broken society that there is such a fellowship of love in which they will find acceptance.

To succeed in evangelism, the congregation must be

conditioned to accept people who are added to the community of faith. Too frequently, in the case of some methods, new believers are not accepted readily into the congregation. But with a congregation being led to participate in friendship evangelism, the spirit of acceptance has already been extended in the confrontation of love.

I am grateful to Art McPhee for this significant work. His insight and practical advice make this work a handbook for the church in friendship evangelism. It is good counsel for sharing the Good News. It is not simply theory, for the author and the congregation which he pastors have been testing the ideas and find them effective. The vision has been shared; it is for us to follow its direction.

—Myron S. Augsburger, *President*
Eastern Mennonite College, Inc.

Friendship Evangelism

The Caring Way to Share
Your Faith

Chapter 1

The Good News People

The headline read, BAD NEWS: GOOD-NEWS PAPER DIES FOR LACK OF MATERIAL. The article which followed began, "As you may have seen, the 'good -news' paper in California recently folded because the editors found that there just wasn't enough good news to fill it. The paper couldn't even print its own obituary because that, of course, was bad news." If good news is really that scarce, the world is in a sorry state. However, there is some good news that is worth repeated announcement.

William Taylor knew that! He was a young Methodist missionary who arrived at the tented city of San Francisco during California's gold rush. Although there was no church, there were hoards of fortune-seekers converging upon the city every day, so Taylor made them his congregation. Each Sunday morning he would stand on a barrel at a busy street corner and shout, "What's the news?" Then, when he had attracted a crowd of the curious, he would tell them, "Brothers, thank God I've got good news for you this morning!"

Taylor's "news" was the story of God's love in Christ, which is never out of date and which bears telling again and again. As Catherine Hankey put it:

> I love to tell the story;
> 'Tis pleasant to repeat
> What seems, each time I tell it,
> More wonderfully sweet.

But why is it such *good* news? Well, it is *good* news precisely because it speaks to the troubled world that could not sustain that California paper. It is news that speaks to the human condition and to the incredibly difficult situations men and women must continually face. It is news that speaks freedom—freedom from guilt, from loneliness, from meaninglessness, and from death.

Freedom from guilt means that men and women no longer have to be weighed down by the burden of conscience. Because Jesus Christ died on the cross, forgiveness is available; and because He rose from the dead, power is available. Through the Holy Spirit, God can turn defeated lives to victorious lives, and that's good news!

Freedom from loneliness means that new friendships in Christ's body, the church, await all who give their lives to Him. These are by no means superficial friendships, however; they are relationships of the deepest kind.

Freedom from meaninglessness means that suddenly life is more than a dead end or an accident. Because God is in the center of the picture and because He has shown that He has a love affair with the creatures He created in His own image, life has a purpose, an eternal one.

Freedom from death means that men and women need no longer live in fear. Death has lost its sting, and there is nothing to dread any more.

The Best News Possible

In February of 1976, I hurried aboard a Piedmont YS-11 for an early morning flight from the Shenandoah Valley to Washington, D.C. There I changed planes for Ohio, where I was to conduct a preaching mission. That day I felt the first effects of one of the most perplexing problems I've faced. At first I did not pay much attention to it. I thought I must be coming down with a cold. My voice seemed excessively loud, but only to me. When I spoke to my audience, I felt like I was shouting into a barrel. Also, my breathing sounded like wind rushing in and out of a tunnel, and the beating of my heart was much more noticeable than before. I assumed the problem was temporary, but it persisted through the weeks and months ahead. Sometimes the loudness of my voice was so distracting, I got a splitting headache. That happened in preaching, invariably, and I would have to mentally argue myself out of quitting in the middle of my sermon.

What did it all mean? Perhaps the Lord wanted me to leave the ministry. If that's what He wanted, I would do it. It would be the worst news of my life, but I was prepared to accept it.

I learned that the cause of the problem was a eustachian tube that stayed abnormally open. The eustachian tubes lead from the oral cavity to the ears. Ordinarily they remain closed except when you swallow or yawn, but one of mine never closed, and caused symptoms that were barely tolerable.

What could be done about it, I asked the doctor. Probably nothing. The affliction was rare, and there was no satisfactory way to treat it. I would have to adjust to it.

Several months later I learned that two Japanese doctors had discovered a way to treat the problem. They had found a simple procedure that had proven 100 percent successful. I was jubilant! I had a need, and now there was an answer to it. It was the best news possible.

This troubled world also has a need, a desperate one, and there is an answer to that need too. It, likewise, is the best news possible. Christ has made atonement for sin, and man can have freedom, therefore, from both its penalty and power.

News Is for Sharing

Like all good news, this news needs to be shared. But not just by preachers. All Christians are called to share it—to be good news people to a lost and dying world.

That was Jesus' message. "The Spirit of the Lord is on me," he said, inaugurating his ministry, "therefore he has anointed me to preach good news . . ." (Luke 4:18). And that was the message Jesus commissioned his disciples to tell, for when Jesus sent them out, they went from village to village "preaching the gospel (Good News)" (Luke 9:6). Likewise, that is the word the apostle Paul used to describe his message. Twenty-three times he indicated that it was good news that he bore. And quoting Isaiah, he described all the followers of Jesus who bear these tidings like this: "How beautiful are the feet of those who bring good news!" (Rom. 10:15).

Why Feet?

Have you ever wondered why Isaiah and Paul singled out the feet of those who bring good news? Most feet are ugly, not beautiful. At least I've yet to see any I could truly call beautiful! No wonder the washing of feet was relegated to slaves in Old Testament times! (See 1 Sam. 25:41.) And the odor! What must it have been like to have to wash someone's feet before the advent of modern deodorants and soaps? No, you see beautiful faces occasionally, but never feet! So why did they single out the feet of those who bring good news? Why not their countenances? Why not their lips or their tongues, for are not those the standard instruments of communicating? Why feet?

Do you remember the time when Jesus began washing the feet of each disciple, and Peter got turned off? Feet washing was the job of a slave. Rabbis could expect many personal services from their disciples in Jesus' time, but for one's disciple to wash one's feet was out of the question. So you can imagine how shocked Peter was when Jesus, the rabbi, began washing *his disciples* feet! No wonder Peter was repulsed! Nothing could have been more humiliating!

However, Paul singles out feet because of their relationship with the term, *gospel*. *Gospel* was originally used in connection with good news about an important battle won, news that was brought to the city by a special courier, a runner. Thus, when Isaiah called feet beautiful, he was probably thinking of the Israelite captives in Babylon when the runners raced from the battlefields to announce that they were free at last. But when Paul thought of Isaiah's words, he envisioned Christians, racing to tell their neighbors, their co-workers, their fellow townsmen, their friends and relatives about the freedom that was theirs through Jesus' victory over sin and death. Paul was thinking of the Good News of salvation, not from a military opponent, but from a spiritual and moral one.

What more beautiful sight could there be than the dust and mud-covered feet of those who came with news of freedom for a captive people? Only the feet of those who share the greater good news of freedom from the bondage of sin and death. So, you may have thought of feet as ugly (and in one sense they certainly are!), but when they are engaged in carrying out the Great Commission, they are beautiful!

Notice that it is *good* news that the feet bring.

Bad News

However, the news presented by many Christians is not good news at all. It is more like *bad* news. Jesus wants to send good news people out into the world, but many of the Christians who have gone out have turned out to be just the opposite. They have gone forth not with an announcement but a threat, not with an invitation but a demand, not with friendly persuasion but with verbal coercion. "Repent now!" their bumper stickers demand. "It is appointed unto men once to die, and after that the judgment." "Heaven or hell? Choose ye this day." And their verbal witness is just about as sharp.

No wonder, then, people view Christianity as negative. No wonder they see Christianity as a system of rules and regulations. No wonder people are tuned out or turned off. There may be occasions when harsh words are needed to crack a hard shell, but more often harsh words are harmful words. They keep people away. Rarely are they winning words.

Harsh words make the gospel sound like bad news, just the opposite of what it is. For, as the apostle John put it, "God so loved the world that he gave his one and only Son, that whoever believes in him shall not perish but have everlasting life. For God did not send his Son into the world to condemn the world, but to save the world through him" (John 3:16-17).

Now, just as God did not send his Son into the world to condemn it, neither does he send Christians into the world for that purpose. Christians are supposed to win people, not frighten them away. They do not condemn, they forgive; they do not assail, they invite.

Howard Hendricks tells about a young man who ran away from home with his girlfriend, because his parents were trying to break up the relationship. But the young man did not know that the day after he ran away, the illness he had been seeing the doctor for was diagnosed as cancer. So while the young man was doing his best to keep from being found lest he lose his love, his parents were doing their best to find him lest he lose his life.

There is a very real sense in which that is the task of the

church. There are millions of people in the world who have a cancer of the spirit called sin, and it is going to kill them unless they see Jesus, the Great Physician, for help. The good news is that Jesus does actually have the cure. It is a cure obtained at great sacrifice, and it is available to all who come to Him. The question is, How does the church get people to come to Him? By threatening? By judging? By coercing? Perhaps on some rare occasions that will work, but the usual way, the Jesus way of winning people is by bringing them good news, not bad—the Good News of God's love.

Eyewitless News

If some bring bad news, others bring the news badly. They are almost completely without tact or common sense. They too are bad news people, not so much because of their message, as because of the way in which they bring it.

Many television stations call their local news program either "Action News" or "Eyewitness News." I am not sure why they cannot be more original. At any rate, "Action News" I can do without. It suggests to me that news must be spellbinding, action-oriented to be worthwhile. "Eyewitness News" I like better, except that too often it turns out more like "eyewitless news," as one magazine writer dubbed it recently.

The Good News is supposed to be eyewitness news too. The apostle John said, "That . . . which we have heard, which we have seen with our eyes, which we have looked at and our hands have touched—this we proclaim concerning the Word of life" (1 John 1:1). Like John every Christian is also a witness to an experience of the love of God in Christ. That means you and me. Our good news is that Jesus Christ has loved us and forgiven us, and He will do the same for all who come to Him.

It is eyewitness news that we have to give, but like TV newscasters, the way in which we present that news often turns it from eyewitness news into eyewitless news. Too many of us are witless witnesses.

David Augsburger tells about a barber who had great zeal for witnessing, but an obvious lack of tact. One day a customer walked into his shop, and in a voice as friendly as you please, said to him, "Hi, what's new?" The barber replied that nothing was new, "except the Good News that Christ died to save sinners," and he added, "that sure includes you." (Neat barb, wasn't it?) The customer kept trying to change the subject, but the barber kept coming at him with "biblical bullets," all of which, as you might expect, missed their target.

When I was in the Navy, I was sharing my new-found faith with a friend. He said that he used to attend church when he was a boy, but there were some ladies in the church who were always badgering him and his sister about whether they were "saved" or not. When they answered in the negative, the response was always an accusing index finger and a threat of hell. "Religion's OK," my friend, now a grown man, said to me, "but don't you get to be like those old ladies. Because of them, neither my sister or I have ever gone back to that church."

Think back to the person who was most influential in your becoming a Christian. Perhaps it was a parent, a close friend, a stranger, or a preacher. Now reflect on how that person was influential in winning you. Was it through a persistent and obnoxious insistence that you become a Christian? Was it through bombarding you with proof-texts? Was it by means of tactless reproofs that you were won?

Every Disciple's Task

In the New Testament we read about a group of people

who were sent out by the church for the specific purpose of preaching the Good News. They were the William Taylors and the Billy Grahams of their day, and the; were called evangelists (or "good newsers"). For example, in Acts 21:8, Luke writes, "Leaving the next day, we reached Caesarea and stayed at the house of Philip the evangelist, one of the Seven" (See Acts 6:5 and 8:5ff.). And Paul says of God's gifts to the church, "It was he who gave some to be apostles, some to be prophets, some to be evangelists . . ." (Eph. 4:11). Likewise, Timothy is admonished in 2 Timothy 4:5, "Do the work of an evangelist. . . ." In each of these instances it would be quite appropriate to translate the word "evangelist" as "good news person(s)." But although it is true that some are special gifts to the church for this task, no one is thereby excluded. The word applies, not just to an office, but an activity, an activity which ought to involve every true follower of Jesus. For every Christian it should be as it was for Peter and John when they told the Jewish court, "Judge for yourselves whether it is right in God's sight to obey you rather than God. For we cannot help speaking about what we have seen and heard" (Acts 4:19-20).

The Story of Four Lepers

In 2 Kings 7, there is a fascinating story about four men who were lepers when Syria was making things miserable for Israel. Samaria was under siege and food supplies had been cut off by the Syrians, so there was famine in the city. Things were so bad, in fact, that the most worthless part of an animal brought outlandish prices, and in addition, there had been at least one incident of cannibalism in the city.

So the four lepers, who were outside the gate of the city, found themselves reasoning, "Why do we sit here till we die? If we say, 'Let us enter the city,' the famine is in the city, and we shall die there; and if we sit here, we die also. So now come, let us go over to the camp of the Syrians; if they spare our lives we shall live, and if they kill us, we shall but die."

But when the lepers reached the Syrian camp, they were amazed to find it abandoned. God had caused the Syrian army to hear the rumble of chariots and horses, the sound of a great army. Thinking the Israelites had hired the Egyptians and the Hittites to rout them, they fled in terror. They fled in such haste, in fact, that they took nothing with them, leaving their tents, their horses, their food—everything. So you can imagine the amazement of the lepers. And you can imagine what they did. They ate, they drank, and they started to carry off the silverware. But then they had second thoughts. "We're not doing right," they said to each other. "This day is a day of good news." So they went to the city and told the king's household (2 Kings 6:24–7:9).

There was good news to be shared, news that affected the lives of an entire city, news that meant the difference between life and death. It was news the four lepers couldn't help but share. There was no way they could keep news like that to themselves. Can a new dad keep the news about his first son a secret? Can an engaged couple keep their marriage plans a secret?

The Problem and the Challenge

Although all of us who are followers of Jesus have good news to share, altogether too often we *do* keep it a secret. The lives, not only of a city, but of millions all over the globe are at stake, yet for some reason, unlike Peter and John, unlike the four lepers, unlike a new dad or newly engaged couple, we have difficulty in sharing the news we have.

Perhaps it is because too often the Good News has not

been presented as *good* news, but as "or else!" news. Or perhaps it is because the Good News has been presented so inappropriately so often. But that is no reason for us to hide *our* light! The alternative to good news presented as bad news or good news presented badly is not to neglect it altogether. Rather, it is to carry out this greatest of responsibilities and privileges aright.

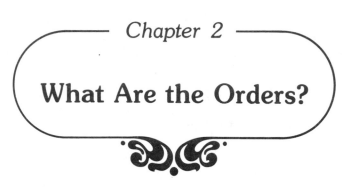

Chapter 2

What Are the Orders?

In our evangelistic efforts, these days, we stress the importance of *methodology* and *motivation*. We say that if Christians are going to be successful in evangelism, they are going to need to be boned-up and psyched-up. They are going to need a program and a push, a system and a shove. Both, we say, are absolutely vital!

And we suppose that if we're doing poorly in our faith-sharing efforts now, if we had to give up these two essential factors for success, we'd have absolute disaster!

Yet, as I read the Great Commission and other New Testament passages relating to evangelism, I find that it is these very things that are most conspicuously missing. We consider them to be, perhaps, the most vital elements of all successful soul-winning, yet Jesus and the apostles hardly mention them!

For me, at least, that is difficult to relate to. Take *method*, for example. It is difficult for me to even conceive of Jesus giving important orders like these without having *something* to say about method. "Make disciples," He says in the Great Commission in Matthew 28, but He doesn't give a clue as to how it's to be done. "Baptizing . . . teaching" give us some help, to be sure, but not much.

What is even more disturbing than that, however, is

the fact that there is nothing much in the rest of the New Testament either. Certain insightful men like Robert Coleman and Paul Little have been able to help us to at least deduce some methodology by examining Jesus' relationship to His disciples and His meeting with the Samaritan woman at the well. But that is not the Bible's primary concern in reporting these things. The Bible describes those things more as happenings, as Jesus in His role of relating to others. The Bible does not capitalize on the inherent methodology that can be seen in those encounters.

The New Testament, of course, does record Jesus' instructions to the Twelve and to the Seventy, but most of those directions sound more like Emily Post than a handbook on witnessing principles. They have more to do with etiquette than with techniques of persuasion.

Punctured Preconceptions

So where do you find in the New Testament the kind of direct methodological treatments of the task of faith-sharing that we have become used to? Where are those stock questions for backing the evangelistic target into an inescapable corner? Where are those four or five magic points that are guaranteed to at once convict and convert the sinner? *Where's the system* Jesus must have put forth?

Not only that, *where's the shove?* Everybody knows that you have got to give people a little push to get them to share their faith! In fact, you've got to give most people a great big push! Else why do we need to have missions rallies and seminars on evangelism and the like? Boned-up and psyched-up—you can't get away from it! Everybody knows that in order to have evangelism you have got to rally people to the cause. That is why pastors and church leaders have had to learn to be such clever guilt-builders with respect to the evangelistic task.

But, although you may search the New Testament from

beginning to end, you will search in vain for the tooth-pulling, for the begging, for the pleading that is employed today in order to get church people to witness. Consider Matthew's account of the Great Commission, for example. Jesus does not have to beg and plead with the disciples to go out and share the Good News. In fact, Luke points out the additional fact that Jesus had to tell them to wait! Nowhere do you find Jesus pleading with the disciples to witness.

So in the Great Commission, and in the New Testament as a whole, these two things are conspicuously absent. There are no clever methods set forth, and there is no clever guilt-building. There is neither system nor shove.

But there is something that makes the absence of those two factors even more disconcerting. It is bad enough that what we have come to regard as so important is not even found in the New Testament. But what is worse is this: while the first century Christians succeeded marvelously in evangelism without ever having had the advantage of a Four Spiritual Laws or books like *Evangelism Explosion*, our success, even with our shelves lined with such helps, has been next to nothing!

Are there, then, other factors that are more important to evangelistic success than these—some that we've been overlooking, some that we can discover from a careful re-examination of Jesus' Great Commission? Let's see.

A Universal Gospel

The first thing Jesus says is, "Go and make disciples of all nations." This construction is almost exactly parallel to one found in Matthew 9:13, where we hear Jesus commanding the Pharisees, "Go and learn what this means: 'I desire mercy, not sacrifice.'" Now, obviously, the important word there is not "go," but "learn." Likewise, in the

Great Commission, the important word is not "go" ("Go and make disciples . . ."), but "make disciples." However, that does not mean for an instant that we should play down the universal implications of the gospel. Some have misused this fact and suggested that Jesus was not, therefore, giving a missionary command. They have suggested that this simply means that "as we are going," we should make disciples, i.e., as we are going about our ordinary affairs. But Jesus' words go beyond that. He did not merely say to go and make disciples, He said, "Go and make disciples *of all nations!*" Or perhaps we could put it, "Go and make disciples of all peoples," which would include all nations, but also all classes, casts, and cultures. There is, in other words, a universal vision for the gospel here, that Matthew, especially, does not want us to miss.

Matthew prepares us very early for this, and it is evident throughout his Gospel, in the events and sayings from Jesus' ministry which he chooses to record.

It is significant, for example, that Matthew, in his geneology of Jesus, indicates that the line of Christ included Gentiles as well as Jews, that it was racially and culturally mixed, in other words. So, included, you find Ruth, for example, and the Gentile prostitute, Rahab.

Then, when you get to chapter two, it is significant that Matthew, alone, records the coming of the Magi, which seems to anticipate an enlargement of God's people.

Then, in the third and fourth chapters, Matthew once more indicates his interest in the universal implications of the gospel in his choice of Galilee as the geographical focal point of his gospel. For example, notice how, in chapter four, he quotes these particular words from the prophet Isaiah: "Galilee of the Gentiles," (v. 15), or you could say, "Galilee of the nations."

Numerous other examples of Matthew's interest in the fact that the gospel would be preached to all peoples could be cited too. For instance, Matthew is the only Gospel writer who tells us that Jesus said, in interpreting His parable of the wheat and the tares, "The field is *the world.*" Likewise, Matthew is the only Gospel writer to indicate, in the story of Mary's anointing of Jesus with ointment, that the gospel would be preached *throughout the whole world.* It is Matthew, again, who reports that Jesus taught His disciples, "You are the light of *the world.*" That does not exhaust the possible illustrations, but it does serve, I think, to show that Matthew did perceive the task of evangelism as a universal one, reaching out to Jew and Gentile alike. In other words, the gospel is for everyone, everywhere. When Jesus said, "Go and make disciples of all nations," you can be sure that He was not envisioning some narrow little ministry that arises as a kind of adjunct to our other activities.

As we've noted, however, more than geography is involved. When Jesus spoke of "all nations," that meant "all peoples." Geographically, that means the world; but socially, it means all sorts and conditions of men and women; and individually, it means the young, the middle-aged, the old, the underprivileged, and the privileged. *That* is the vision, and that defines the *real* extent of our task.

For Jesus, that meant associating with all manner of people, even though He was often criticized. The Pharisees, for example, could hardly take the fact that Jesus befriended some of the people he did. And there can be no doubt that others felt the same way. What must people have thought of His choosing a tax collector as one of His inner circle of twelve disciples? What must they have thought of His associating with Samaritans and prostitutes? What must they have thought when He actually rendered Himself unclean by touching a leper? No one ever came to Jesus and was not welcomed. No one was ever shut out of His life. For Jesus, the universal implications of the Good News meant far more than geography. It meant putting Himself in the midst of the most trying, difficult circumstances imaginable. He meant reaching out to every hurt. And that is what it must mean for us too.

"Go and make disciples of all peoples" means that wherever God has called us, be it here or abroad, we must be prepared to place ourselves right in the middle of the tensions, the alienation, the aches, and all the rest of society's ills, for it is just there that the reconciling presence of Christians is needed most of all. Bringing lost men and women back in touch with God, each other, and themselves is not an easy job. It means involvement. It means risk. It means putting yourself right in the middle in order to call men and women to the Christ who came to put an end to alienation once and for all. Every disciple of Jesus Christ is called to befriend the good, the bad, and the ugly of this world. If we really love the One who so loved the world that He sent His only Son to die for it, then we will be willing to lay our lives on the line as well.

This invading rather than inviting, this go rather than come mentality means that Christians who are serious about Jesus' Commission cannot be satisfied with reaching out to a lost world institutionally. That can never be sufficient. They will feel constrained to also reach out personally. Making disciples of all peoples goes far beyond evangelism by proxy, merely putting money for missions into an offering plate. It means injecting ourselves into the anguish and the brokenness of people's lives, because we care, and because that is what salvation is all about—making people whole again, recycling the wasted lives of men and women who are in the same condition we were once in.

That, to me, suggests that one of the chief priorities of local congregations should be to make a drastic shift from the accepted evangelistic strategy of recent generations. Congregations must somehow move away from being "come" structures to being "go" structures.

Make Disciples

That brings us to the main verb itself: "make disciples." There is only one other place in the New Testament (Acts 14:21) where you find this verb used like this, in the active voice, but you do find the noun, "disciple," used many times, especially by Matthew and John. Matthew uses it seventy-four times, for example.

What can we notice about the term? What does it mean to "make disciples?" Certainly, one of the things that it means is implied in the requisite of baptizing in Jesus' Commission. Whatever else making disciples means, it must include baptism, that is attachment to and identification with the triune God. It means relationship to a Person. It seems to me that that is the clear implication of "baptizing them." While it is true that baptism also symbolizes entrance into and identification with the body of Christ, with the New Humanity where differences of race and culture and class are transcended, the primary meaning is identification with the Person in whom those differences disappear! So that we do not call men to a denomination or to distinctive doctrinal stances or to a style of life primarily (which is not to negate their importance, however), but we call men, first of all, to identification with Jesus Christ!

Jesus did not call people to a religion, or a creed, or a cause, or a philosophy, or even, primarily, to a way of life. He called men, first of all, to Himself. And when we call men to discipleship, let us always remember that we are not calling them to our local congregation, our hermeneutic, or anything of the sort. We call men and women to one thing only and that is to Jesus! How often has evangelism in practice consisted merely of an invitation to come to our church on Sunday morning? How often has it been in practice merely a call to champion the cause of the poor, or of peace? Well, certainly there is nothing wrong with calling men to help the poor or to work for peace, and there is nothing wrong with inviting someone to church. But that is not evangelism. Evangelism is calling men and women to Jesus. Discipleship means relationship.

Now, that is different than the Jewish concept of discipleship. When the apostle Paul, for example, was a disciple of Gamaliel, his attachment was based on his respect for the knowledge, the teaching and the reputation of the great rabbi. His attachment to him was on that level. And that is the way it always was between the Jewish rabbis and their disciples. But Jesus' disciples were not attached to Him in that way at all. For a long time, not only did they not even understand His teachings, but they didn't like what they thought they did understand! No, they were attached to the Person! It was a faith relationship! It was based on Jesus Himself, not His ideas or His teachings.

So discipleship means *relationship*, first of all. But it also means obedience and cost—"teaching them to obey everything I have commanded you." When a man became the disciple of a rabbi in Jesus' day, as with Jesus' disciples, it meant a giving up. So we read that when Jesus called Peter and Andrew, "at once they left their nets and followed Him," (Matt. 4:20). Likewise, when He called James and John, "immediately they left the boat and their father and followed him," (Matt. 4:22). There was cost involved.

There are, of course, many passages you could use to illustrate this, but when Jesus' disciples gave up all that had before seemed indispensable to them, it was a different thing than when the disciples of the other rabbis did. The situation was not really the same.

Sometimes the rabbinic disciples gave up a great deal, but they also knew that a great deal more would come to them because of the people's dependence upon the Law and, therefore, upon the teachers of the Law. And even though they were giving up certain things for the time being, soon they would be rabbis (teachers) themselves, with students thronging to them. And with all of the privileges of their position as rabbis, they would be well fixed.

But Jesus' disciples did not have that mentality. At least not for long. Because it soon became apparent that for disciples of Jesus, the goal of becoming as good or maybe even better than their rabbi was out of the question. They did not see themselves as potential equals with Jesus or as Jesus' successors. They would be like Jesus, but they would never be His equals or His superiors in popularity, acclaim, wisdom, or anything else. In the words of Jesus Himself, in Matthew 10:24, "A student is not above his teacher, nor a servant above his master; *it is enough for the student to be like his teacher, and the servant to be like his master.*" So, for the disciple of Jesus, discipleship is not the first step with greater things to come. Merely being a disciple is the fulfillment of his destiny! The rabbinic disciples hoped to some day master the Law. But Jesus' disciples wanted only to be mastered by Jesus.

Just as it was for the Twelve, then, our relationship is always to be one of disciple to Master. He always remains our living Lord. And that is the relationship to which we call men. Thus, our job in making disciples is not primarily to be the faithful mediators of Jesus' insights. It is not to pass on to the world the enlightened thoughts of a great teacher. But it is to call men to costly obedience to Jesus Himself.

Jesus is not our rabbi, but our Lord! And that means witness *to Him* is the task to which we are called. When you look at the message of the early church, that comes through again and again. Their proclamation was witness to Jesus and not primarily the passing on of His insights. They called men and women *to Him.*

I want to repeat, though, this was not merely a call to belief, but also to obedience. Making disciples goes far beyond calling men to intellectual assent. One of the failings of modern evangelism is that it has called many to belief but few to obedience. In the words of Jim Wallis, "The question has become, do we believe *about* Christ, rather than are we willing to forsake all and follow Him!"

That is, in part, what the great emphasis on *methods* has done. It's stripped down the message so that all that is left is a call to easy believism. "Faith in Jesus is all that's needed," we say. It's one, two, three, four, five—just like that! But we do not tell the people on our prospect cards that, in the Bible, "faith" always means faithfulness! It means costly allegiance! It means radical discipleship! It means putting your life, your livelihood, your all at the complete disposal of Jesus!

Too many of us, I'm afraid, have been hoodwinked into believing that method in evangelism is everything, but look at the methods! What are they designed to do? They get people to sign a card or pray a prayer, and that's okay, but when the focus is there, instead of seeing that as the first step in a life of discipleship, then it is nothing less than a tragedy! Think of how many people may be lost with decision cards in their pockets, because they've never really had a relationship with Jesus. All they've ever really had is an intellectual acceptance of Him.

So, it seems to me, that instead of methods, we'd better be talking about personal obedience *for ourselves*, because that is the only way I know, of passing on the concept of discipleship so that others will really catch its significance. The early Christians succeeded because they knew what discipleship meant in practice. The first Christians not only talked about the Holy Spirit, they were empowered by Him. The first Christians not only talked about reconciliation, they were reconcilers themselves. The early church not only talked about Jesus, they followed Him daily in life.

Without those things, you see, you may have evangelism but you don't have the gospel. The Good News is that Jesus is alive, and that means we have something *personal* to share. A witness isn't somebody who merely repeats what somebody else has told him, or who has mastered the art of getting a message across. A witness is someone who has experienced what he's talking about. The love of Christ becomes known to others through Him, because it is a reality in His own life.

Chapter 3

Catching Men Alive

It was a pleasant evening in the spring of A.D. 28. The nearby town of Capernaum was alseep, but from the boat you could still see it clearly, serenely silhouetted against a shimmering, starry wonder of a night sky. The lake was a starry wonder itself and seemed to mirror the sky, but its lights were the torches of fishermen, seeking to attract a good school within the toss of their nets.

Simon was gazing intently into the torch-lit water around his boat, when an age-old call came from an approaching craft.

"Any luck?" It was his partners, James and his brother John.

"Nothing James. What about you?"

"The same. Let's work our way toward the harbor. Dawn will be upon us before long anyway, and the fishing there can't be any worse than it's been out here in the deep waters."

"Agreed," said Peter.

But when at dawn they came to shore, both boats were still empty.

Later, while the men were washing their nets, they saw Jesus of Nazareth coming toward them. As usual, there was a crowd thronging about Him. The atmosphere was electric. It had been that way ever since He had come to town. He took up his teaching, and each day hundreds of people gathered to hear him speak. But it was no wonder! He was exciting to listen to! Some thought He was a prophet. Some thought He might even be the long awaited Savior of Israel.

When Jesus got to where Simon and James and John were washing their nets, He stepped into Simon's boat and said to him, "Will you put out a little from shore?" Simon was only too happy to comply—now his empty boat was good for *something* at least! So he sat in the boat with Jesus, while He taught.

Then, when Jesus had finished speaking, something almost laughable happened.

"Put out into deep water," He said to Simon. "Let down the nets for a catch."

Simon answered, "Master, we've worked hard all night and haven't caught anything."

But Simon wasn't the kind to disappoint anybody as important and popular as Jesus, so he added, "But because You say so, I will let down the nets."

The rest of the story you know—how they let down the nets and caught so many fish that the nets actually began to tear, and they had to signal James and John to come in the other boat to help them. You know, too, how Peter was so overwhelmed and astonished by the miraculous catch that he told Jesus he wasn't worthy of his association. "Go away from me, Lord," he said, "I am a sinful man."

Luke doesn't tell us what Peter's companions in the boat said, or what his partners in the other boat said. But he does say that they, too were astonished by the size of the catch.

A New Kind of Fishing

However, what I want to call to your attention is the reply of Jesus to Simon, which is one of the most significant things He ever said. I believe it is as important for us as it was for Simon. It is a statement that sums up what should be every Christian's vocation in life, and clearly establishes where our priorities need to be. Furthermore, it gives unique insights about faith-sharing.

Notice what Jesus said to Simon and how the others took it as a signal to themselves as well. He said to him, "Don't be afraid, from now on you will catch men."

Then, says Luke, "they pulled their boats up on shore, left everything and followed Him."

What does it mean to catch men? What does it mean to follow Jesus and have fishing for men as your stated vocation in life? What does it mean to leave everything else in order to take up that as priority number one?

It is a call that is familiar enough to all of us who are Christians, is it not? "Come, follow me," Mark records Jesus as saying, "and I will make you fishers of men." There were Simon and his brother Andrew, and James and his brother John, going about business as usual, and along comes Jesus with his marching orders (or shall I say fishing orders?). But what is "catching men?" Have you ever seriously thought about the way in which Jesus put this commission to them, and ultimately to us?

Literally Jesus said, "From now on, you will be catching men *alive.*" Translators do not usually bring that over into the English for a very good reason. When you do so, it takes the emphasis off the "men." In the Greek that doesn't happen. But that is what Jesus literally said, "From here on out, you will be catching men alive (or for life)." Let's consider some implications of this.

A New Agenda

First, when we heed Jesus' call to become fishers of men, we acquire a new agenda. *"From now on,"* Jesus says, *"you will catch men."*

There are times in life that stand out from others, because they mark a turning point, a new direction, a new departure that completely transforms the future.

For Paul it happened on the Damascus Road.

For D. L. Moody it happened in the back room of a shoe store.

For C. H. Spurgeon it happened in a little church called the Artillary Street Methodist Chapel.

They met Christ, and their life's agenda was completely changed.

So it is in the history of a people. The crossing of the Red Sea marked such an occasion for Israel. For Colonial America it came with George Washington's victory at Yorktown. For Australia, New Year's Day of 1901 was such a turning point. The Commonwealth was proclaimed, and suddenly the people's agenda was drastically changed.

In addition to his experience on the Damascus Road, another such time in Paul's life came when he was preaching in Corinth. The Jews had become very vocal and belligerent in their opposition to Paul, so according to Acts 18:6, Paul shook out his clothes in protest and said to them, "Your blood be upon your own heads! I am clear of my responsibility. From now on I will go to the Gentiles."

Those three little words, "from now on," meant a complete change of agenda for Paul. No longer did he concentrate his efforts on the conversion of the Jews, his own people. He turned his efforts instead to a ministry to the Gentiles.

Jesus' death and resurrection marked such a turning point too. They meant the end of His earthly ministry as servant, and the beginning of His heavenly ministry as King. So He makes this statement to His accusers at his trial: "From now on the Son of Man will be seated at the right hand of the mighty God" (Luke 22:69). And again, you find those same three words, "from now on."

Likewise, when Jesus uses those three words and says to Simon, "From now on you will catch men," He is clearly indicating that Peter's agenda is changing. No longer will he be spending his time catching fish; now he will be catching men. From now on things will be different for Peter.

Has your decision to follow Jesus made a difference in your agenda? Or is it still so full of items like homemaking, shopping, cooking, writing, selling, planning, organizing, studying, teaching, sewing, discipling, decision-making, phoning, and so on, that there's no time left for witnessing? I'm afraid for many of us, that is the case.

And at times even our church work is more program than passion, more human activism than divine obedience, more externalism than internalism, more work than worship.

But the answer, of course, is not to flee from program to passion, but to a *new* program. As someone has pointed out, a passion, however good, is only a passion until it expresses itself in a program.

That is why, unlike other religious leaders, Jesus did not present His first disciples with some kind of mystical idealism, but with a brand new agenda: healing the sick, feeding the hungry, visiting the imprisoned, clothing the naked, preaching good news to the poor—all as a part of the task of catching men alive and for life. So the fact is that we have not really heeded the call of Christ until we have given ourselves over to His program, as well as to His person.

A New Aim

When we heed Jesus' call to become fishers of men, we also acquire a new aim. "From now on you will catch men." The emphasis is on the word men: "*Men* you will catch alive," Jesus says. Men instead of fish.

When Jesus spoke of *catching* men, the disciples understood His words to be synonymous with *fishing* for men. This was language that Simon and Andrew and James and John understood well. They were only four of scores of fishermen from the towns around Lake Galilee. The historian Josephus, who was once governor of Galilee said that there were about 330 fishing boats used on the lake. The fishing industry was to the towns there what the steel industry is to Pittsburgh. Even the names of the towns indicate that.

For example, Bethsaida meant "house of fish." Tarichaea, another of the lakeside towns, meant "the place of salt fish." So Jesus' imagery about catching (or fishing for) men was readily understood by the Galilean disciples.

The kind of fishing Jesus was talking about was net fishing. When we transfer imagery like this to our day, we are at a bit of a disadvantage. We automatically think of angling (with a rod and baited hook). But Jesus was speaking of net fishing. If we understood this properly, we would have a much-needed corrective to what often passes for evangelism these days. Faith-sharing today is almost always more analogous to angling than to net fishing. It has an entirely different aim.[1]

For one thing, angling is a solo effort, while net fishing is an enterprise of partners. When Peter and Andrew's boat began to sink, because of the weight of the catch of fish, they immediately called upon their partners for assistance. Evangelism, too, is basically a partnership endeavor. Witness is not the function of individuals primarily, but of the brotherhood together. In his unity prayer, Jesus asks the Father to bring His disciples to complete oneness, "to let the world know that you have sent me and have loved them even as you have loved me" (John 17:23). Similarly, Jesus says in John 13:35, "All men will know that you are my disciples if you love one another." Such unity and love catches the attention of the world, in other words, and convinces it of the authenticity of Jesus' mission. Thus, Christian community is essential to the proclamation of the Good News. What good would it have done for the Peters and Pauls to call men to Christian community if there had been no such visible community in view? What good would it have done for them to say that Christ had broken down the walls between Jew and Gentile, slave and freeman, male and female if there were no demonstrable proof of it? What point would there have been in calling men and women to an *invisible* new humanity? This, then, is the light set on a hill, the visible communion of God's children living together in unity and love.

Secondly, angling depends upon trickery and violence, while net fishing is a much more natural method. Fishing with hooks and lines involves the violent removal of fish from their surroundings, and it also employs deceit. However, net fishing is quite another story and involves catching fish together and within their normal context. This has several implications for evangelism.

To begin with, it casts serious doubts upon forms of evangelism that utilize entrapment. There are methods of visitation evangelism which are highly regarded and broadly used among evangelicals that have doubtful biblical underpinning. Their roots seem closer to Madison Avenue than the New Testament. The motive is right, but the methods are questionable. Furthermore, it is extremely difficult to train more than eight to ten percent of a given congregation to use any direct-confrontation approach. George Peters, long-time professor of world missions at Dallas Theological Seminary, told me that those percentages were verified in research both in the United States and abroad. On the other hand, he said, in a typical congregation an additional twenty-five percent could be expected to become involved in friendship evangelism. Why? Well, because in the approaches involving clever quick-sell schemes, many Christians have the uneasy feeling that they are insensitively forcing a hard-sell gospel on unwilling, unwitting listeners.

Would it not, therefore, be much more natural and effective to share the Good News out of a relationship of trust, based on friendship? Such an approach may take longer, but almost invariably it is better received, and its results are more lasting.

Not only that, but usually it is assumed that the Christian must yank the new convert out of his cultural environment into the context of a particular congregation (which usually means no more than a particular worship service), even though he may feel utterly ill at ease and out of place, like a fish out of water. Reflect upon your own experience, for example. How many times have you witnessed the failure of such an approach? How many times have you seen new converts brought into a congregational setting and simply left there with the expectation that a little indoctrination and a lot of preaching would guarantee a mature and well-adjusted disciple? But what inevitably happens, instead, is they get frozen out. Instead, why not disciple the new Christian in his own neighborhood, among his own friends and relatives through a small group and a sustained personal relationship? Why not involve him with Christians of similar background and with some of the same perspectives and needs? By all means, help him to identify with a congregation where he feels he can really worship, but don't just leave him there!

"But do churches really grow when such methods are employed?" you ask. Certainly they do! And they grow qualitatively as well as quantitatively, which is vital for healthy churches. That, by the way, is a very striking feature of the Acts account of the growth of the early church. There is no lack of emphasis on numbers— numbers are obviously important; but, at the same time, comment is always made on the qualitative side as well. Acts 9:31 is just one of many examples that could be cited: "Then the church throughout Judea, Galilee and Samaria . . . grew in numbers" *(quantitative)*; but, also: "it was strengthened; and encouraged by the Holy Spirit, (lived) . . . in the fear of the Lord" *(qualitative)*.

A contemporary example of such a church is Gospel Temple in Philadelphia. Gospel Temple was a successful Pentecostal congregation that, in 1970, resolved to change its whole style of ministry. It did so by dropping all of the regularly scheduled church activities except the Sunday morning worship service; instead the members began meeting in small groups in homes, where real caring and nurture could take place, and where Christian witness could take place more naturally. Quality growth didn't happen all at once, but within four years they had to have two Sunday morning worship services, and within six years there were over thirteen hundred involved in the Sunday services. The "Home Meetings," as they called them, grew to more than fifty, with from twelve to twenty persons participating in each of them.

Thirdly, the angler fishes merely for sport, while the net fisherman fishes for a living. The angler is interested only in trophies; the net fisherman, on the other hand, needs to fish in order to sustain himself and his family. So it is with the church. The church vitally needs the gifts God has to give her. The church cannot exist without them. The success of the church's ministry depends directly upon those gifts, which God always gives through individuals. Thus, the church does not fish for fun or trophies, but for survival! The purpose of gifts is to produce fruit, and without fruit, the church must wither and die.

Finally, the angler is interested only in the catching, while the net fisherman is also vitally concerned with the keeping. Friendship evangelism, evangelism that cares, is not a mere exercise in scalp-hunting. Its interests are long-term. When a man or a woman is won to Christ by a caring disciple, he or she perceives his commitment to that new Christian to be a permanent one. Even commitment to follow-up will not be enough; it must be follow-through!

Basically, then, the difference between fishing with a net and fishing with a hook has to do with our respect towards human beings as persons. There is, I suppose, nothing particularly wrong with fishing for fish with a hook and line, but it is wrong to catch men that way! Oliver Wendell Holmes, in *The Banker's Secret* said, "See how he throws his baited lines about, and plays his men as anglers play their trout." He didn't know it, but he was giving a perfect description of much Christian evangelism, evangelism that focuses on the catching, rather than the keeping, evangelism that is more interested in trophies than in persons, evangelism that hooks people by clever methods and forces them violently into positions they are not ready to assume willingly, evangelism that *uses* people, as an angler uses his bait.

In chapter eight of his book, *The Compleat Angler*, Izaak Walton described how to use a frog:

> Thus use your frog: put your hook . . . through his mouth and out at his gills, and then with a fine needle and silk sew the upper part of his leg with only one stitch to the arming-wire of your hook, or tie the frog's leg above the upper joint to the armed wire; and in so doing, *use him as though you loved him.*

True New Testament evangelism does not *use* people. Jesus was thinking of net fishing when He said that we are to be fishers of men. Net fishing is different altogether. The motives are different and the methods are different.

A New Allegiance

When we heed Jesus' call to become fishers of men, we also acquire a new allegiance. Luke says that the disciples left their nets and followed Jesus.

That act suggests several things. It suggests that catching men now took priority even over their own livelihoods. The most important pursuit for them from now on would be catching men. And the Greek indicates that this was to be a permanent vocation for them.

Their decision to follow Jesus further suggests that Jesus needs to be sovereign in our lives. We are to be following Him, doing His will; and doing His will means catching men alive (or for life). And what a life there is in Christ! The former life just does not compare with it. We are more vitally, more intensely alive than ever before in the One who has called us, and it is to that same quality of life that we bring our catch.

Chapter 4

Caring Evangelism

Thirty young people returned from an afternoon canvass of homes in their community. They were excited as they entered the "campaign headquarters" in the basement of a local church.[1]

"I got twelve decisions for Christ!" said one vivacious and attractive girl. "I never dreamed it could be so easy!"

"I got six," said one young man. "I could hardly believe it. I would just introduce myself and say, 'God has a wonderful plan for your life,' and it seemed like I had 'em. They didn't have any hesitation at all about praying the prayer like I thought they would . . . except a few."

"That's how I found it too," said another. "They just followed right down that 'Romans Road,' one, two, three—just like that!"

"I used the Kennedy method," said another. "That question about knowing for sure if they'll go to heaven if they die today was a real clincher, as far as I'm concerned." He laid a stack of decision cards on the secretary's desk.

A few days later, when follow-up began, and those who were called upon were reminded of their decisions, almost none showed any further interest in the gospel. Some even seemed indignant! What had happened?

Actually, it is what *didn't* happen that ought to concern us. There are a number of important considerations that

Christians often overlook in their efforts to win persons to Christ, and some are quite alarming.

Persons As Objects

For instance, sometimes persons are treated as mere objects or "souls" to be cornered and captured. Each victim is little more than another notch of the evangelist's spiritual tomahawk. His evangelistic activity might be more accurately called "scalp hunting" than "soulwinning." However, Jesus didn't die for "scalps"; He died for persons. Therefore, the caring evangelist is concerned for persons: their backgrounds; their hurts; their needs. He believes he has no right to talk to another person about his relationship to God until he, himself, has developed a relationship with that person and/or until he has sought and received the Holy Spirit's permission to encourage his prospect to receive Christ. His conception of his task is that of a servant-witness, not a salesman (and certainly not a high-pressure salesman!).

Instantaneous Conviction of Sin

Caring evangelism also recognizes the need of a genuine conviction of sin. Usually that takes time. We are sadly mistaken if we believe that conviction of sin is ordinarily an instantaneous thing. Scripture is one of the most powerful tools for conviction that the Holy Spirit uses, but we must always remember that it is He who does the drawing and not the mere recitation of the Word. And usually the Spirit does so in His own time and through the word of a friend.

So just saying the words, "All have sinned and come short of the glory of God" or "All we like sheep have gone astray" must never be considered as some kind of magical incantation resulting in —poof!—the shattering of the victim's ego. It does nothing of the sort! What it does do is

to convince the person that if he has a need, it is for
sanctification only. The talk about the need for forgiveness probably will not really register with the person at
all, because he has no conception of the depth of his sin,
but sees it, rather, as a collection of minor blemishes that
can be covered by the formation of more acceptable patterns of behavior.

Repentance Minimized

Another danger of "care-less" evangelism is that repentance is often minimized. Yet, repentance is absolutely essential to genuine conversion. Said Menno Simons, one of the Dutch Anabaptists, "If you want to be
saved, your earthly, carnal, ungodly life must be re-
formed. For the Bible teaches us nothing but true repentance. If you do not repent there is nothing in heaven or on
earth that can help you, for without true repentance we
are comforted in vain. Whenever true repentance and the
new creature are not there, man must be eternally lost;
this is incontrovertibly clear."[2] Caring evangelism takes
seriously the lostness of the lost, and is not content to lead
persons to a superficial faith that is a false faith.

Cheap Grace

Likewise, we must be careful to be honest about the
cost of discipleship. Too often Christianity is presented
simply as an alternative life style, an adventure, an escape, or the ultimate "trip." While there may be an
element of truth in such pictures, it is not the whole truth.
To omit any mention of the cost involved in being a
disciple of the Lord Jesus is not friendship, but dishon-
esty. That is why I also have serious misgivings about
Christian television programing that leaves the impression that Christians are always good-looking, middle class
Americans: ever youthful; never fat; never troubled by

disappointment, loneliness, financial failure, sickness, acne, or anything else for that matter! That is why, as David Augsburger has put it, "The spiritual landscape is strewn with the ruins of those who 'laid the foundation,' but could not finish." If Jesus felt it was vital to point out the cost (see Luke 14:25-35), should we neglect it?

False Assurance

Caring evangelism is also ever-so-cautious not to foster false assurance. If a decision is made *about* Christ rather than *for* Him, for example, a man or woman may proceed under the assumption they are saved even though their lives never exhibit any evidence of conversion (see James 2:19). Years later, when they are asked about the basis of their assurance, they point to that magical moment when they "prayed the prayer" or "came forward," but the fact that there is no reference whatever to what God has done indicates that someone did not explain the "decision" properly. There was no *real* decision for Christ at all, and there was no understanding of their need to take up their cross "daily" (Luke 9:23).

Premature Pressure

Sometimes God's timing and our zeal can be at odds. Insensitivity to God's Spirit and to the friends we are seeking to make for Him often results in our pressing for a decision too soon. I have encountered many persons who have become antagonistic toward Christianity as the tragic consequence of such an unfortunate and over-anxious insistence. One young man told me: "I was pressured into making a decision I did not want to make, after which I was asked if I felt like a Christian. When I said I didn't know, I was accused of not believing God, because if I had confessed my sins, God had promised to be faithful in forgiving them. But I didn't really feel I had any sins

that were bad enough so that I needed to be forgiven!"
This young man felt he had been tricked into something
superficial and false. He was humiliated and incensed,
and he vowed to me that nothing like that would ever
happen to him again!

Now, of course, there are many helpful guidelines for
presenting the gospel which are available to the Christian. Many of these methods are quite useful, and I would
not, for a moment, want to detract from the positive
contribution they make. But they must never be used
impersonally or mechanically. Also, the caring evangelist
ought to attempt to compensate for their weak points or
omissions. While "care-less" evangelism may result in
some real conversions, there may be many more who are
turned against Christianity. Others may conclude that
Christianity is no more than a shallow, meaningless gimmick. Still others may go through life with a false assurance of salvation, and to hell with a decision card in their
pocket. What is our responsibility in the light of this?
Shall we conduct our evangelism haphazardly? Or will we
see that discipling is not quite as simple as, perhaps,
we've thought?

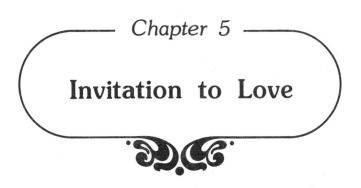

Chapter 5

Invitation to Love

Love is the motivating force behind evangelism that cares. It is the love of Christ reproduced in men and women like you and me. "We love because he first loved us," wrote John (1 John 4:19).

Jesus told the disciples that the world would know He had sent them, by their love. Love is the mark of my disciples, He told them. John echoed that, indicating, "Everyone who loves has been born of God and knows God. Whoever does not love does not know God, because God is love" (1 John 4:7, 8). Inevitably that love must show itself in evangelism. It will show itself in other ways too, of course—in service, for example. But the love of Christ in a man or a woman cannot help but reach out to those who are without hope and without God. As Paul put it, "Christ's love compels us" (1 Cor. 5:14).

Effective evangelism needs to be built upon love for two essential reasons. First, love meets a perceived need in men and women everywhere. Secondly, the God we proclaim is love in His very nature (1 John 4:16).

Love Meets a Perceived Need

The search is on— for new energy sources, for new ways to weed corruption out of government, even for a vaccine for tooth decay, I read the other day. Man is a restless and searching creature, always looking for new cures, new commodities, and new comforts.

But one of the objects of his searching fills all three of those needs, and that is love. Take the search for *new cures*, for example. New drugs, new surgical techniques, new ways of preventing disease are all great, but love is a greater key to sound health than all the other discoveries of medical science put together. As Karl Menninger has said of mental disorders, "Love is the key to the entire therapeutic program of the modern psychiatric hospital."

Or take the search for *new commodities*, the importance of which is greatly exaggerated in a capitalistic society such as ours. Of all the commodities that are presently at our disposal, or will be in the future, none will ever supplant love in importance. As someone has said, "Love is a commodity without which no individual or civilization can long endure."

Or take the search for *new comforts*. All other comforts are nothing compared with the encouragement of love. As Paul wrote of the comfort that Jesus gives, "If you have . . . any comfort from his love," (Phil. 2:1).

It is true! Whatever else man is searching for at any given point in history, the rediscovery of love is always the best treasure to be found. Love meets in many strange and wonderful ways the most deeply perceived needs of man.

Most men and women are not looking for religion, nor do they often have the time or inclination to ask themselves questions about the meaning of life, nor do they perceive themselves as miserable sinners in need of forgiveness. But most men and women *are* looking for love.

They are not interested in religious propaganda (tracts), nor are they interested in answers to questions they are not asking, but they are interested in love.

We can't win most people by scaring them with talk

about impending judgment, and we can't win most people through reasoning, no matter how eloquent an advocate we may be—unless they can see that behind the warnings, and behind the arguments, is our genuine love for them.

"There is only one way not to be won over by love," Napoleon once said, "and that is to flee from it." Is not that how we were won over to Jesus? It wasn't that *we* loved God, as John reminds us in 1 John 4:10, "but that he loved us and sent his Son as an atoning sacrifice for our sins." That is why we gave our hearts to Christ, not because God sent us a tract or an argument or threats, but because He sent us His Son and His love.

Even Animals Respond to Love

Have you ever noticed how even animals respond to love?

Once, a soldier returned home after a long tour of duty overseas. When he opened the gate and started down the walk to the home where he had grown up, he saw his old friend, the German Shepherd that had been his faithful companion all through his teens. Instantly, the soldier raced up to the dog, threw his arms around him, and said, "It's sure great to see you again, pal," and the dog responded with warm affection. However, when the young man was inside, his parents told him that this dog wasn't his boyhood pal at all. His dog had died while he was away, and this was another dog.

"We kind of wish old Shep *was* still with us," said the young soldier's father. "This new dog is not nearly as amiable or predictable, and he's utterly vicious with strangers."

When the young man went outside again, naturally he was more cautious about the new dog, and the dog sensed it and immediately bared its teeth and snarled. It had sensed the young man's love; it could also sense his suspicion.

I heard about a man one time, who worked for a dairy farmer, but he treated the cows meanly. When eventually he changed jobs, the farmer discovered that milk production increased significantly. The only way the farmer could account for it was that the new hired hand treated the cows more kindly.

There is a sense in which even plants respond to love. We talk about people who have green thumbs. That means their plants respond to their care. But while we often use that figure of speech, we all know that it really has nothing to do with their thumbs at all, and ultimately, even their botanical know-how is secondary. Their plants grow, because they love what they cultivate, and the care they give them reflects it.

Now, if animals and even plants respond to love, then you can be certain that people do. There is, of course, no guarantee of how great the immediate response will be, but nearly always there will be some noticeable response, and in the end, love will prevail. There will be some who will flee, of course, but not only will most persons respond to your love, you will find that they are actually on the lookout for such love to respond to!

E. Stanley Jones wrote about a hostile crowd he faced on a speaking tour in India. They were chanting and waving black flags. But he spoke warmly to them and tried his very best to demonstrate the love of Christ in his speech. In the end not only did the crowd respond to his obvious love for them, but they gave him one of the black flags to take home as a souvenir!

That is why John's description of Christians as people who know how to share love is so pertinent to faith-sharing. You became a Christian because of the love of God in Christ. You also became a Christian, in part at least, because you saw and experienced that same love in some Christian acquaintances along the way. That's how you knew the good news of God's love was for real! That's how you knew Christianity was for real! Because you witnessed it. You experienced it. "All men will know that you are my disciples if you love one another," Jesus said (John 13:35). It convinced you; it will convince others too! Love unlocks the hearts of men.

God Is Love

That is the first reason why this love John speaks of is vital to evangelism. The second is this, that God loves, and is, by nature, love.

Someone has said that the greatest evangelist in history was not Billy Graham, nor Billy Sunday, nor D. L. Moody, nor George Whitefield, nor even the apostle Paul. The greatest evangelist in history was Jesus Christ. And nothing was more crucially central to the message of Jesus than love.

Reflect for just a moment. Why did Jesus come into the world? To bring judgment? To pronounce us all guilty? To condemn the world? No, the Bible says, "God did not send his Son into the world to condemn the world, but to save the world through him," (John 3:17). And the Bible says in the verse immediately preceding that one, that that act was an act of love: "For God so *loved* the world that he gave his one and only Son . . ." (v. 16). Love is what the Incarnation is all about.

So it follows that Jesus' invitation to us to be good news people is an invitation to love. Not just an invitation to talk about love, but to practice it. As Dave Wilkerson likes to put it, "Love isn't something you say; love is something you do." God didn't send us a tract from heaven describing His love; He sent us a living demonstration of it—He sent His Son!

I wonder if we have even begun to understand the significance of that, and of the fact that God is love (John 4:16). It explains a great deal about this universe in which we find ourselves, and it explains a great deal about life.

For one thing, it explains why God created this world and we humans in the first place. There can be no other explanation for His creating a world, which He knew would be such a heartache and so much trouble to Him. The explanation can only be that creation was an essential act of God's nature. If God is love, then He cannot live in a vacuum. Love is not love without recipients.

For another thing, love explains why man was free to rebel against God. God didn't create puppets or robots. He created creatures capable of responding freely to the love He wanted to give.

The fact that God is love also accounts for salvation, of course, which is the greatest manifestation of all of that quality of God. Thus, at the very heart of the evangelistic message is the fact of God's love. Love, of necessity, must find a remedy for sin and the Fall. When the soul is sick, love, of necessity, must find a cure.

The Essential Unity of the Church

All of this raises a crucial question. If love is central in evangelism, why has there been so much division in the churches? Luke wrote of the early church, "All the believers were one in heart and mind" (Acts 4:32). But that has hardly been true since that time!

Do you remember how the apostle Paul gloried in the fact that the church's chief feature was its unity. Christians, since they know only one Lord, one faith, and one baptism are all members of one another, according to Paul. And in the church, therefore, there is neither Jew nor Genitle, slave nor free man, male nor female. All such distinctions disappear in Christ. That was what Jesus

Himself prayed for in His prayer for the church in John 17, you will remember. His prayer was that "they may all be one." And He fully expected that prayer would be answered, and that there would be "one flock, one Shepherd," as He put it on another occasion.

All the New Testament images of the church indicate also that such is to be the case. For example, there cannot be many bodies of Christ, there can only be one body; and there cannot be many new Israels, but only one New Israel; and Christ does not dwell in many new temples, but only in one.

That would seem to leave no room for petty bickering and rivalries between churches and church groups. That would seem to leave no room for the squabbling and fighting that has been so prominent in the churches down through the years. Yet, honesty demands that we recognize that there have been divisions and conflicts from the beginning. From the very beginning rifts have scarred Christian brotherhood. That, despite Paul's beautiful theological statements, has always been the case, and even Paul himself had to deal with it.

So how do you bring the two together—the theological necessity and the actual reality? Was Paul wrong about the nature of the church? Was Jesus' prayer never really answered, despite His expectations? Were His predictions untrue? Was the church, as Luke describes it in Acts 4:32, only a temporary fluke? If so, then a great deal of the wind has been knocked out of the Good News we seek to share!

But, no, the church, like the Christian, is becoming what God intends for her to be. She has not arrived, but is in process. She will not be seen in her fullness until after Jesus Christ returns. The divisions *can* be accounted for.

Let me illustrate. The New Testament talks about the Christian in three tenses. First, it talks about the fact that we have been saved, as in Titus 3:5, where Paul says, "he saved us"—past tense. Secondly, it speaks of salvation as something that is presently going on, as in 1 Corinthians 1:18, where we read that "to us who are being saved, it (i.e., the message of the cross) is the power of God"— present tense. Finally, we read that salvation also has a future aspect, as in 1 Peter 1:5, where Peter says that we are guarded by God's power through faith for a "salvation that is ready to be revealed in the last time." So the New Testament does not recognize any such thing as a full-grown Christian in this life. We are not, according to the New Testament, mature Christians, but maturing Christians. We are in process. We are becoming. And only when we are finally glorified, will we be all that God intends for us to be.

So it is with the church. The church, too, is in the process of becoming what God intends for her to be: one flock with one Shepherd.

That is the explanation, but that doesn't mean that we pass by working at the divisions now! We must never allow ourselves to be consoled into apathy by the promise of the future. We must, rather, respond with positive action! For the sake of our witness, we desperately need to work at the divisions now! The divisions can be explained, but they cannot be excused!

And, really, it *is* possible to overcome many of the differences in the churches. We can at least do so in our attitudes toward each other, by recognizing that we have a common purpose in this life. Each denomination, each group within the church wants to do the will of the Lord. Each of us wants to move toward the promised future when we *will* be one flock with one Shepherd. And to the extent that we have that purpose in common, we are already believers with one heart and soul. Let us at least understand that! Let us know that *in terms of direction and commitment* we *are* one. And let us prove the authenticity of the love we show toward others, by demonstrating that it exists supremely within the church. Let's act as though we are one by exhibiting what Jesus said would be the evidence that would convince the world of the truth of our claim to be His church—our love for one another, even in the midst of temporary differences.

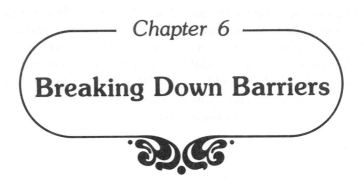

Chapter 6

Breaking Down Barriers

Witnesses on Ice

A friend of mine, who comes from a community of declining churches, says that God has called him to work among His "frozen people." But when it comes to spreading the Good News, God has "frozen people" everywhere. Even in churches that are popping with excitement and growth, many are afflicted by a curious paralysis that keeps them from sharing the faith.

Pastors are not the exception. One pastor told me, "You know, I have been preaching about the need to spread the gospel for years, but when I come down from my pulpit, I'm just like many of my people. I want to witness, but I cannot bring myself to do it. I look for opportunities to talk about Jesus, but even when I find them, unexplainably I freeze up."

During an evangelistic crusade I conducted recently, another pastor told me that participation in the crusade was his congregation's entire evangelistic program for the year. He was not happy with it he said, "But how can I lead them in something that I have never been able to bring myself to do?" In tears he told me, "I have not once led a soul to Christ."

This strange paralysis is a paradox that is difficult to

explain. It is as if Walter Cronkite, with the best news story of his life to report, froze up on camera. It is as if a new dad forgot to tell his co-workers that his first son had just been born. It is as if the news media failed even to mention that a long and terrible war had finally come to an end. How do you explain whatever it is that keeps Christians from sharing their Good News? What prevents them from talking about it even when, inside, they are aching to do so?

The phenomenon is even more strange when you realize that there have been times when the churches have apparently had almost no difficulty with this issue. For example, evangelism never seemed to be a problem for the early church—at least not major enough to be highlighted by the New Testament. Nowhere do you find the apostles pleading, scolding, or organizing for evangelistic activity. Nor was personal evangelism a problem among Reformation groups such as the Anabaptists. Nor has it been an issue during any of the great revivals. In such settings evangelism just happens! And it happens effortlessly, spontaneously, automatically! Read about some of these periods. It is exciting! A problem? "How can we help but speak?" they asked. They could not help themselves!

Nevertheless, we *do* have the problem. Right now Satan is employing all sorts of hindering devices to make Christians feel uncomfortable about sharing their faith. And he seems to be succeeding! What is the matter? What can be done about it?

Creeping Universalism

In *Death in the City*, Francis Schaeffer laments the decline in missionary interest. He says that it must be explained by one of two things: a loss of compassion; or a lost sense of the lostness of the lost. I am sure that he is right on both counts, but the latter observation is especially on target. In a sense there is still a lot of compassion left in the churches. Some relief agencies are having to expand their ministries to handle the funds that are coming in. Volunteers for disaster assistance are still in good supply. And most churches work hard at making some impact on the social needs of their communities. But there is an alarming new lack of compassion for those in a lost spiritual condition. It is not that Christians don't care, however. Rather, it is connected with a growing tendency toward universalism. More and more Christians are doubting the doctrine of hell. And the result, of course, is that faith-sharing becomes less vital.

But to the apostle Paul it was vital! And one of the reasons why was his conviction about the impending judgment. "For we must all appear before the judgment seat of Christ," he wrote (2 Cor. 5:10). Then, in the very next verse, he shared what that meant for him in the present: "Since, then, we know what it is to fear the Lord, we try to persuade men."

It is difficult to argue, then, with Francis Schaeffer, who calls a spade a spade, when he concludes: "If we are Christians and do not have upon us the calling to respond to the lostness of the lost and a compassion for those of our kind, our orthodoxy is ugly and it stinks. And it not only stinks in the presence of the hippie, it stinks in the presence of anybody who's an honest man. And more than that, I'll tell you something else, orthodoxy without compassion stinks with God."

Three Kinds of Barriers

But although a creeping universalism and, with it, a loss of compassion for the unsaved is certainly a part of the dilemma, most evangelical Christians are confronted by even more formidable barriers to faith-sharing, barriers that usually fall into one of three categories: first, the barrier of limited ability; secondly, the barrier of limited courage; and thirdly, the barrier of limited power. Let's examine these three barriers to witnessing.

Mary R. Hooker said one time that when Jesus found the Galilean disciples, they were mending their nets, and she added, "The majority of Christian people are always washing and mending their nets; but when Jesus comes along, He tells them to launch out into the deep and let their nets down. That is the only way to catch fish."

Well, one of the most frequent reasons you hear as to why Christians do not let down their nets is their limited fishing ability, and you usually hear it expressed in one of two ways.

Limited Speaking Ability

First, there are those, like Moses, who say they cannot speak. Do you know what the number one fear in America is? It is not financial problems, nor illness, nor bugs, nor snakes, nor heights, nor even death. Rather, the fear Americans mention most often is speaking before a group.

That same fear carries over into the area of witness. Nothing is more embarrassing than having something to say and not knowing how to say it.

A limited ability to verbalize scares more Christians out of the urgent task of sharing their faith than anything else, perhaps.

Preachers can talk about the obligation to witness until they're blue in the face, do all sorts of clever guilt-building, and the people in the congregation will agree right down the line, but their lack of confidence in their ability to speak will still render them mute every time.

Limited Intellectual Ability

But it is not just limited speaking ability that keeps

them from sharing their faith, but also, limited intellectual ability. At least that is their perception. What if somebody asks me a question I can't answer? What if they think I sound dumb? What if they notice that I'm not very educated? This can be just as big a barrier as limited speaking ability.

But let me share a secret. It's scary for me to get up in front of a group of people too, even though I have to at least once a Sunday. That is especially true if I haven't had lots of time for preparation. And I get worried about my intellectual powers too. If I had given serious thought, when I was invited to come to my present church, that I would be facing college professors week after week, not to mention the dean of a seminary, and occasionally, a college president (or two as was the case on one occasion), plus several authors—if I had thought about that very seriously, I wonder if I wouldn't have been quite happy to remain a country preacher in Pennsylvania, as I'd been until then.

But I want you to notice in 1 Corinthians 2:1-5 how Paul came to Corinth:

> When I came to you, brothers, I did not come with eloquence or superior wisdom as I proclaimed to you the testimony about God. For I resolved to know nothing while I was with you except Jesus Christ and him crucified. I came to you in weakness and fear, and with much trembling. My message and my preaching were not with wise and persuasive words, but with a demonstration of the Spirit's power, so that your faith might not rest on men's wisdom, but on God's power.

Was it any different for Paul? No, Paul says that when he came to Corinth to share his faith, he came in weakness, and with fear, and with his knees knocking! The great apostle Paul! It sounds hard to believe, doesn't it? Yet, that is his testimony. Why do you suppose he felt weak?

Why do you suppose he was fearful? Why do you think his knees were knocking? The first reason was Paul's limited speaking ability. And the second was his limited intellectual ability. Paul says, "I did not come with eloquence or superior wisdom." It wasn't that Paul didn't have both, however. Paul *was* an eloquent man, and he was an intellectual giant. But when Paul went about the task of sharing his faith, he was, in a sense, limited—by the strange culture, by what must have seemed like a very simplistic message to the philosophically astute Corinthians, and by certain other factors too. But God wasn't interested in eloquence. God wasn't interested in his ability to do intellectual sparring with the Greek philosophers. He only wanted him to share an utterly simple message about Christ and His cross.

Undoubtedly Paul must have thought, What are these philosophers and wise men going to think? (No wonder his knees were knocking!)

But God wasn't interested in Paul's ability. He was only interested in his availability, and that applies to you and me too. Even if you are right about any personal limitations you may have, no matter what they may be, it doesn't matter. The primary thing is not your abilities, the primary thing is you—your availability.

But what about the barrier of limited courage? What about the fear of not knowing what to say, or of being rejected?

What to Say

Let's look at them.

First, the fear of not knowing what to say. Now of course, there are all sorts of witnessing schemes on the market today. They are meant to assist Christians in explaining about man's need and God's plan of salvation. But sometimes they have scared persons more than helped them. Understand, they have helped many, but there are many who have not been helped either. However, notice the apostle Paul's simple plan.

Paul decided that rather than try to compete with the philosophical speculation of Corinth, he would just present the simple message about Jesus and His crucifixion. He would do it without apology, without embarrassment, without rationalization.

Likewise, you don't have to be able to give an eloquent speech in order to share your faith. And although it may be helpful, you don't need to memorize an elaborate "plan of salvation." All you need to be able to do is to introduce people to Jesus, as Andrew did with Simon, and as Paul resolved to do. The primary thing is not to introduce people to a plan, but to a Person.

Remember the story of Naaman? Naaman, you will recall, was a leper. He was commander of the army of the king of Syria. He was held in high favor by the king, and he was a national hero. But he was a leper. You can well imagine that that must have been a devastating thing for Naaman. He had achieved a great deal in his lifetime, but now fate had struck him an irreparable blow. Leprosy had invaded his body, and he was finally face to face with an enemy he couldn't defeat.

But in Naaman's household there was a little maid who waited on his wife. She didn't know anything about leprosy, of course, except for its tragic results. She didn't have the slightest idea what caused it or how it could be cured. She couldn't offer any home remedies or any theories about how to deal with the dread disease. But she did know a man who could give Naaman the help he needed. So, little as it may have seemed, this little maid passed on the one bit of information she had. She said to her mistress, "Would that my lord were with the prophet who is in Samaria! He would cure him of his leprosy" (2 Kings 5:3). That was all she knew, but it was enough. She couldn't cure leprosy, but she knew someone who could, just as we know Someone who can cure the leprosy of sin.

Witnessing is *every* Christian's responsibility and winning men and women to Jesus is *every* Christian's privilege. Where did we ever get the idea it was just for a few extroverts? Where did we ever get the idea that you need some special expertise? Where did we ever pick up the notion that unless you have got a gimmick, you can't win souls?

Have you ever introduced two people? Have you ever said something like, "This is my friend, Bob. Bob helped me when I was in trouble, and I think he can help you too." When you boil it down, isn't that all witnessing essentially is? It doesn't take a course in public speaking—only a little love.

Fear of Rejection

But what of the fear of being rejected? Well, there is no promise that that won't happen. The Bible indicates that it happened many times to Paul. And it happened even to Jesus (John 6:61-66).

Aware that his disciples were grumbling about this, Jesus said to them, "Does this offend you? What if you see the Son of Man ascend to where he was before! The Spirit gives life; the flesh counts for nothing. The words I have spoken to you are spirit and they are life. Yet there are some of you who do not believe." For Jesus had known from the beginning which of them did not believe and who would betray him. He went on to say, "This is why I told you that no one can come to me unless the Father has enabled him." From this time many of his disciples turned back and no longer followed him.

But the Bible also says that the fields are white unto

harvest, and that means that there are also many who are ready to hear, and who *need* to hear the Good News. Otherwise their lives and their futures will remain a shambles. A little rejection is a small price to pay when you consider the alternative.

But here are some clues for working at this fear:

1. Begin by sharing your faith in settings where you do feel comfortable. Do it with other Christians in a small group setting. Share with people you know are sympathetic, about what the Lord has been doing in your life.

2. Try going with someone as a silent witness. Become used to the witnessing context by simply accompanying someone on that task.

3. Spend time with persons who talk about their faith freely, persons who seem to have mastered their fear.

All of these you will find to be of real help. They incorporate sociological and psychological principles which will help you to overcome many of your fears faster than you would have imagined.

Limited Power

Then finally, there is the barrier of limited power. Paul went in weakness, into a strange culture, not knowing what to say or just how to say it. He had the same fears that we have. In one sense, he was just as powerless as we are. But in another sense, he had the greatest power in the world at his disposal—the power of God through His Holy Spirit. As Paul himself put it: "My message and my preaching were not with wise and persuasive words, but with a demonstration of the Spirit's power."

Really, all of us are powerless when it comes to passing on our faith. No amount of eloquence can give another person faith. No amount of intellectual persuasion can do it. No amount of boldness can create faith in an unbeliever. No words. No methodology. The success or failure of any evangelistic effort is the direct result of the presence of God the Holy Spirit and our willingness to honor Him and give Him complete control of the witnessing situation. Faith is not our gift; it is the gift of God. But God's method is always a man or a woman—a person who is at His disposal. That person is you.

So you see, none of these things we think are barriers to effective witnessing are barriers at all. Effective witnessing doesn't depend upon any of these things. Upon the contrary, the only real hinderance to sharing your faith is self. When ability is more of a factor than availability, then your witness is affected. When your own skin is more important than those who are still lost, then your testimony will suffer. When calling attention to yourself is more important than calling attention to Christ, then you shall surely fail. But there is only one barrier that stops you—yourself. The others are all illusions of an introspective preoccupation, one that, with God's help you can overcome. Therefore, trust God—He will guide you in your witnessing, guard you in your witnessing, and give you power for witnessing. Like Paul, above all else, desire to give God the glory, and you will discover that you— even you—can witness with confidence!

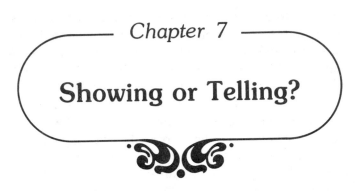

Chapter 7

Showing or Telling?

Love in Action

Over the years parents have been advised that what they
communicate to their children by example is more important than what they communicate to them verbally. Not
many would argue with that. After all, that is just an
application of a truth that has been recognized for generations. "Practice what you preach," one old adage put it.
"Actions speak louder than words," said another.

But that poses a bewildering question. If this truth
really has been recognized for generations, why have
Christians been so reluctant to apply it to the task of
faith-sharing? Most books on witnessing have emphasized
telling when, if anything, the weight ought to be on the
showing. The result has been a lop-sided witness to the
world: long on words, but short on deeds.

That is not the Bible's emphasis, however. The Bible
does not minimize the necessity of sharing the faith by
word of mouth, but it also emphasizes that words need to
be fleshed out to have effect. You may be a silver tongued
orator like William Jennings Bryan or as smooth a talker as
the best used car salesman in town, but the most eloquent
language of all is the language of love. As the apostle Paul
put it, "If I speak in the tongues of men and of angels, but

have not love, I am only a resounding gong or a clanging cymbal" (1 Cor. 13:1). Thus, while it goes without saying that showing does not take the place of telling, nevertheless, as Paul indicated in his statement about love, declaration without demonstration is meaningless.

It is easy to talk about the love of God, but what convinces people of its reality is not your words alone, but also your way. If you demonstrate by the way you live and relate to others that the love of God has become a reality in your own experience, *then* you have something that is hard for people to walk away from. As someone has written, "The greatest proof of God's love is a life that needs His love to explain it."

There are many ways in which such love is demonstrated. For example, I have Christian friends in the community where I live who take persons in crisis situations into their homes; who work faithfully in the local prisons; who are volunteers in the county hospital; who collect and clean soap from motels in Virginia to be sent overseas for folks who cannot afford such luxuries; who minister to the mentally handicapped; who provide meaningful activities for the elderly; who share lawnmowers, appliances, even living facilities in order to have extra money available for relief and other special ministries; who have systems for finding out about their neighbors' special needs; who provide transportation for persons who require assistance in their grocery shopping, or who have no way to the doctor's office or church—I could go on endlessly. All this I see going on around me right now, in the town where I live!

But love is not demonstrated just among the down and out, the distressed and destitute. There are thousands of little ways to show love in our everyday contacts with fellow workers or students, with relatives, with friends and neighbors, with salesmen, with department store clerks, with fellow riders on the bus or subway, and the list goes on. Just listening, for example; how important that can be for a man or a woman with a burden—just to have someone available who cares enough to hear their hurt or their concern! Affirmation, counsel, prayer, a helping hand, a touch, a "faithful wound" as the Book of Proverbs calls it—all these are also vitally important ways of proving to the world that not only are we Jesus' disciples, but that the Father did, indeed, send Him on a mission of mercy to lost mankind.

It Is What You Are That Tells

The reason why your words and your actions must always coincide, of course, is that it is what you *are* that affects the lives of others. I am not likely to take anything you say very seriously unless I can have assurance that it arises out of conviction. And I am not likely to take you seriously unless I sense that the ideals you articulate so well are more than dreams and have something of the stuff of reality about them. And I am not going to take you seriously either, if I have any inkling that you are not authentic, if I suspect that you are not what you say you are. If you say you are a rose, and I smell a skunk, then can you blame me if I allow your words to flow in one ear and immediately out the other?

In Amy Carmichael's *Edges Of His Way*, the fragrance of Christians is described as being like light, always visible; like love, intangible and invisible, yet always recognizable. "It is what we *are* that tells," she says. There's a poem I like by an unknown writer, which expresses the same thought in a bit different way:

> The Gospels of Matthew, Mark, Luke and John
> Are read by more than a few,
> But the one that is most read and commented on
> Is the gospel according to *you*.

You are writing a gospel, a chapter each day
By the things that you do and the words that you say,
Men read what you write, whether faithless or true,
Say, what is the gospel according to *you?*
Do men read His truth and His love in your life,
Or has yours been too full of malice and strife?
Does your life speak of evil, or does it ring true?
Say, what is the gospel according to *you?*

Evangelism and Christ's Presence[1]

This brings me to the heart of what I want to say in this chapter. This "fragrance," which Amy Carmichael speaks of, and which the apostle Paul also speaks of in 2 Corinthians 2:14-15, depends entirely upon whether Christ, by the indwelling Spirit, is present in our lives. If He is not an abiding reality to us, then there must always be something inauthentic about our message. We will not be able to adequately demonstrate it by our lives, and there will never be the ring of truth in our declaration. Just the opposite will be true. Evangelism must be incarnational to be authentic; it must be based upon personal experience! The living God must be shown to have become flesh and to be now living in us.

When we think of the remarkable success the early church had in carrying out Jesus' Great Commission, we are likely to think of the key to that success as somehow having a vital connection with His *initial* statement, "All authority in heaven and on earth has been given to me," (Matt. 28:18). But I have the conviction that Jesus' *concluding* statement about his presence is just as important: "And surely I will be with you always, to the very end of the age" (Matt. 28:20).

Certainly our inability in the twentieth century to duplicate the results of the first century church has not been due to a rejection of Jesus' claims about his authority, has

it?—at least not in evangelical circles. Nor has it been due
to a failure to take the Great Commission seriously. The
vast number of books on the market on the subject of
evangelism ought to convince us of that. But could it be
that one significant reason why we've been so impotent in
our witness is that we've failed to grasp the importance of
this final assurance Jesus gave His disciples?

Certainly the churches of our day have not been turning the world upside down, as the early churches did.
Indeed, it might be more accurate to say that the world
has in many instances been turning the churches upside
down! So, to be sure, there is something wrong! So, I have
the deep conviction that an important part of the explanation has to do with our witnessing to a second-hand Christ
of doctrine, rather than a first-hand Christ of experience.

In the first chapter of his Gospel, Matthew reminds us
of words spoken by the prophet Isaiah:

> "The virgin will be with child and will give birth to a son,
> and they will call him Immanuel"—which means, "God
> with us" (Matt. 1:23).

And in the final chapter of his Gospel, Matthew reminds
us of some of Jesus' final words:

> "And surely I will be with you always" (Matt. 28:20).

What are the implications of that statement that He is
with us, and, specifically, what are its implications for
evangelism?

A Form or a Force?

In Paul's second letter to Timothy, he talks about the
cold, formal, orthodox Christian who holds "a form of
religion," but denies the power of it (1 Tim. 3:5). Could it
be that this describes us? Could it be that we have been so
interested in the Christ of doctrine that we have missed

the Christ of experience? Could it be that our failure to effectively communicate the faith has been related to a certain unreality about our witness?

Let me make it personal. Is Christianity *for you* a relationship, or is it merely a religion? Is it authentic, or is it synthetic? Is it a "force," as Moffatt translates it, or is it merely a "form"? What are you building on, traditions passed down the centuries from apostolic days, cold-storage concepts that you have inherited and accepted almost without thinking? Or does your faith rest instead upon a Christ with whom you have daily fellowship? Have you settled for "the real thing," as the Coke ads put it? Have you settled for a relationship that you can call "mine" personally? Or have you settled for something less—a counterfeit, a second-hand faith? I believe if there is to be any hope of reaching the world for Christ, our Christ is going to have to be a first-hand Christ of experience, not a second-hand Christ of doctrine. We are going to need to move Christ from the cabooses of our lives to the engines of our lives.

Walt Whitman was listening to a learned astronomer's speech one night, but soon he became restless and slipped outside the stuffy lecture hall for a breath of fresh air. The scholar's speech about the stars had bored him, and his charts had bored him even more, until as Whitman himself put it, "I wandered out into the night and experienced the stars themselves!" However, many of us have never even thought of wandering out into the night. Instead, we have been content to remain in the stuffy lecture hall, pouring over our theologies, and commentaries, and charts, all of which are valuable, but which, alone, keep faith second-hand.

No wonder, then, the world is suspicious of the Christ we offer it. People can sense that there's something wrong, that our faith is not genuine, that it's unauthentic!

It's a far different Christ we are lifting up than John lifted up. John said that that which we have seen, and heard, and touched, *that* we declare to you (1 John 1:1-3). But there is nothing of that personal testimony in the witness of many Christians today, either in their speech or their actions.

Voltaire once said of his relationship with Christ, "We salute, but we do not speak." I'm afraid there is too much of that in the churches these days. Grown up in a religious atmosphere, in a religious country, there are many who have learned to be polite to Christ: they salute. But they have never learned to know Him: they do not speak. There are many who, acknowledging Christ's authority, would support any effort to carry out the Great Commission, but they have never caught the *real* significance of Christ's promise to be "with" us.

It is because of that very danger that Luke points out that even though Christ told the eleven to go make disciples of the lost, He told them to do something else first. They were to go, yes; but, first of all, they were to wait. Wait for what? For the promise of the Father, the coming of the Holy Spirit. That is *how* Christ would be with them, you see—through the indwelling Spirit. Thus, behind the fire and the glow, behind the power and the glory of the early church was direct, personal fellowship with God. Is that any less true for the church in the twentieth century? Even today, what could be more important to personal evangelism than that?

The evidence that Christ is with us is in our changed lives. The apostle John said in his First Epistle, if you aren't living what you proclaim, then you have no right to say it is your experience. If you aren't living Christ, then you don't know Him. If you aren't living Christ, then you can't authentically declare Him. If you aren't living

Christ, then all your words, no matter how eloquent, are going to sound phony to the world (and they will be phony!). You'll be peddling a counterfeit; you'll be dealing in unreality. For the only true testimony to Christ is the testimony that comes from a personal relationship with Him.

Do you remember how Jesus puts it near the conclusion of the Sermon on the Mount in Matthew 7? Do you remember how He described men and women who called Him Lord, who prophesied in His name, who cast out demons in His name, who did many wonderful works in His name, as, nevertheless, having something vitally wrong with them? None of these fine things they were doing counted at all, because the most important fact of all was missing in their lives, the fact of a vital relationship with Him. "I never *knew* you," Jesus says!

Thus, if the resurrected Christ is not a living reality for us, we are proclaiming a false gospel, for the Good News that we proclaim is not dead news, nor tired news, nor even old news. It is living news (God-with-us news!), the exciting personal news that the Jesus who came as a babe to Bethlehem is today, every bit as much as He was then, "God with us," that although He was crucified and buried, nevertheless, He is now alive!

Of course, when you say something like that, you'd better be able to prove it. A sermon is not going to be enough. If, like John, you say that you have had a personal encounter with Christ, you'd better have the changed life to show for it, a life charged with Christ's presence, demonstrating the love of Christ—irrefutable evidence that He really is with us!

Here is evangelism at its highest, based not upon somebody's method but upon personal experience, based not upon rumor but reality, based not upon speculative views but spectacular news, based not upon words alone, but also upon deeds, based not upon a theoretical abstraction but upon the living God become flesh and now living in us—Christ with us, both now and to the end of the age!

Chapter 8

Earning the Right to Be Heard

They left with great fanfare. There was a commissioning service in their honor. There was a special banquet. There were articles in the church papers. There were glowing predictions. But when the young couple returned from their jungle mission outpost three years later, there were no converts, no church services, not even many significant contacts to report about.

On their next furlough, three years later, the couple told of numerous new contacts among the tribesmen they had set out to win. And they were able to report that they were finally getting a grasp of the strange language these people spoke. However, there were still no converts, and, still, there were no services.

The home church could not understand it. This young missionary couple had remarkable abilities. Both were bright, exceptionally talented, committed, responsible—what could the trouble be? Why weren't the members of the tribe to which they had gone being won to Christ? Why were there still no church services?

Finally, however, in the eighth year, good news came. Practically the whole tribe had become Christians. And they had begun, almost immediately, to evangelize a sister tribe down river.

The home church naturally wanted to know how such a

drastic change had come about. What had the missionaries been doing wrong? Why did it take eight years for a breakthrough? What new strategy had they devised? But the answer they got was not what they were expecting. The missionaries had not changed their strategy at all. The young couple had gone on with their task just as they had before. What made the difference, they said, was that they had now learned the language well enough and lived in the jungle long enough to have developed rapport with the tribe. A relationship had been built, and now there was trust.

Your Deepest Relationship

Someone has said that your greatest witness is your deepest relationship. That is something that needs to be stated over and over again. It is absolutely essential that we be reminded of that truth. Yet, it is commonly overlooked. For many, faith-sharing is something that you do quickly, almost spontaneously. There is not the time for developing relationships. There is no attempt to identify with people.

But when Jesus sent out the seventy-two to proclaim the news of the kingdom, He gave them instructions that necessitated their identifying with persons. He told them to stay in the homes of those among whom they worked. And He told them to eat their food. This required more than a casual association with the people. They could not obey Jesus' instructions and remain apart and aloof.

In the area where they were to share the Good News, there were many Gentiles, and, possibly, some were hosts to the seventy-two. What would it have meant for a Jew to live in the home of a Gentile? Would Jesus have expected them to eat the Gentile's unkosher food? At any rate, Jesus' assignment must have meant considerable adjustments for the seventy-two, but remember that

Jesus wasn't asking of them something He hadn't done Himself. "The Word became flesh, and lived for awhile among us," said John. Just think of the adjustments that required! What must it have meant for Jesus to leave the eternal courts of heaven and identify with us in that way—to take on human flesh; to take on our infirmities; to become weak; to suffer and die? What did it mean for Him to leave heaven and take up residence in decadent human society? Yet, not only is that what happened, but Jesus' whole pattern of ministry showed that this is the only truly effective way of reaching men and women with the Good News.

We must never allow the fact that it is *good* news that we bring to delude us into thinking that people are automatically going to be all ears to our message. We have to earn a hearing, which necessitates building relationships. And to build relationships, you must associate and identify.

As Easy As A, B, C

What is required? Well, it's as easy as A, B, C, but, unfortunately that's *not* easy! "A" stands for acceptance. "B" stands for benevolence. "C" stands for caring.

Acceptance

First, you need to accept those you hope to reach. That, of course, doesn't mean that you condone their wrong actions or attitudes, but it does mean that you respect them as persons, that you respect their cultural peculiarities, and any other uniquenesses. The struggle Peter had accepting Gentiles is a struggle we still face today. The questions in those days concerned such things as ceremonially clean foods versus unclean foods, special Sabbath observances, and the problem of accepting uncircumcised persons as full members of the body of

Christ. More recently, the questions have had to do with such things as jeans, men with long hair, and new forms of worship. Superficially, the questions seem different; however, fundamentally, they are the same. They all have to do with cultural and traditional hangups. However, salvation has nothing at all to do with cultural uniformity. It doesn't have to do with one's dress; it doesn't have to do with one's speech patterns or vocabulary; it doesn't have to do with one's racial or national background—none of these things! Salvation is dependent upon faith alone, on committing one's life to Jesus as Lord. Culture, tradition, life style are often enriching things. They may even reflect a biblical sensitivity to stewardship or modesty, but they are not the criteria for participation in the body.

I have often wondered how often we let our cultural hangups get in the way of accepting a brother or sister who has decided to cast their lot with Jesus. I am convinced that it happens far more frequently than it should, and I am further convinced that we, in the churches, have not really worked very hard at overcoming it.

Benevolence

Secondly, you need to love those you hope to reach. The building of relationships depends on acceptance first, but there must also be benevolence. Benevolence is more than kindness; it is a sincere, heartfelt desire to promote the happiness of others and the disposition to be instrumental in bringing that happiness about. It is more than an act; it is an attitude. More than two hundred fifty years ago, Butler put it this way in a sermon: "If there be any affection in human nature, the object of which is the good of another, this is itself benevolence, or the love of another." Not only is such an attitude the great need of the hour in this self-seeking age, but it is utterly crucial in earning the right to be heard.

One reason for the crowds that followed Jesus wherever He went was the people's awareness that He loved them. Just as His acceptance of them was apparent when He risked censure by associating with tax collectors, prostitutes, lepers, and the like, so, also, His love for them was apparent in His refusal to turn His back on anyone who came to Him—the poor, the lame, the blind, the possessed, whoever had need. His compassion for a hungry crowd, His tears for a city, His refusal to condemn a woman caught in the act of adultery all demonstrated, too, that He deeply cared about the welfare and happiness of others. The evidence of Jesus' benevolent attitude toward all men and women comes through again and again in the four Gospels.

Caring

Thirdly, you need to care for those you hope to reach. For some, caring for those who have need is only a matter of duty, but biblical caring is the overflow of a benevolent heart, one that really loves people. True love for your neighbor always translates into action. Caring *about* people is never enough; you need to care *for* them! Because God loved us, the Word became flesh (John 3:16); and as with His love for us, so it must be with our love for others.

Many Christians, however, have trouble getting a handle on that. They want to find ways of translating their love into action, but either they can't find ways to do it, or else it doesn't come off authentically.

The first of these dilemmas is mostly a matter of working at it, I think. A woman I know became aware, one summer, that her little girl had become extremely frustrated, because there was never any expression of appreciation for the many little duties she was expected to perform around the house. The mother felt it was important to teach her daughter to take responsibility, so she was assigned chores such as emptying the waste baskets, dusting, and drying dishes. However, the mother had never considered the importance of affirming and thanking the child—until a friend brought it to her attention. "But which things do I pick out to thank her for?" she asked, when she became aware of the need. She wanted to show she cared, but she didn't know how.

Her problem, of course, was that she had never had a pattern of showing gratitude. It was not nearly as difficult to find ways to show it as she thought it would be once she began working at it though. And neither is it difficult for you and me to find ways of showing our neighbors and casual acquaintances that we care for them. It boils down to this: not being afraid to try.

Now, I want to concentrate on the second dilemma, that of overcoming the feeling that our expressions of caring will be perceived more as duty than love.

At first our efforts to express the love we have for others *will* seem to be more duty-motivated than love-motivated. That is simply because our first efforts at demonstrating that love will be very conscious efforts. What we are endeavoring to do will be very much on the surface of our thinking. It will not have become a natural thing, so, of course, we shall have that perception of it! However, when that happens, we need not worry; that feeling will be gone soon enough.

Do you remember your first attempts to drive an automobile? I remember mine very well. I remember the grinding of the gears as I attempted to coordinate the movement of the shifting arm and the pressing of the clutch pedal. I remember the jerks when I applied the brakes too swiftly or failed to shift smoothly into gear. I remember how carefully I watched the edge of the road, so that I would stay properly within my lane. However, that was soon enough all a thing of the past. Before long there was no grinding of the gears, nor were there any jerks. Before long I found that I could gaze far down the road to see what was coming, and I could do so without the slightest uneasiness about staying in my lane. No longer was I tense about my driving. Now, it had become second nature. Now, I could really enjoy it.

So it is with almost every endeavor in life. What is accomplished in the beginning only by conscious effort, becomes in the end an enjoyable and natural experience.

For example, take the youngster with his piano lessons. He plods through his finger exercises and elementary arrangements with real doubts about the value of what he is doing and about the eventual outcome. Before long, piano practice becomes sheer tedium to him, and he begs his parents to allow him to give up. He debates with them about the stewardship of their money, the shortness of his fingers, and the strictness of his teacher, but his parents convince him in the end to stick with it for just a little longer. After awhile he discovers that the lessons are going a little better, and soon he even begins to enjoy them a little. Within a year or two he grows to enjoy playing so much that he just naturally gravitates to the piano during his free moments.

Our love for our neighbor is a gift from God, something that emerges as a response to his unmerited favor towards us. But the outward expression of that love is the result of a pattern (or habit) of caring that we cultivate with God's help. It *does* seem more duty-motivated than love-motivated at first. Naturally, we have our doubts about what we are doing. Of course, we are concerned that it won't come off authentically. But as we work at outwardly expressing our benevolence, all that will change.

Summary

To put it all together, then, our best opportunities for Christian witness come as the result of relationships of trust that have been built up over a period of time. Most of the time people are not automatically going to give ear to the message we want so badly to share with them. But as they come to know that we accept them, love them and are anxious to demonstrate that love in tangible ways, they will begin to open up.

Chapter 9

Easy Lessons in Conversation

Some years ago, Halford Luccock wrote an article in *Christian Century* which he called "Easy Lessons in Conversation." The article focused on conversational styles and, at the end, offered some sage advice. The little essay was more amusing than instructive, but the title, "Easy Lessons in Conversation," has always stuck with me, because I have often wished there were some pointers for Christians who want to witness.

To witness is to certify the truth about something from personal knowledge or experience. There are two ways to do it: by our lives; and by what we say. Both are needed, of course. Telling, as we have seen, means nothing without consistent demonstration. Jesus' credibility lay largely in the fact that he was a living demonstration of everything He taught. But righteous living that is unaccompanied by the proclamation of the Good News is just as empty. In the words of a once-popular song, "they go together like a horse and carriage."

I have a friend who has always insisted that letting his light shine is enough of a witness, but he's as wrong as he can be. Christianity cannot be absorbed without teaching any more than physics can, or chemistry, or biology, or grammar, or anything else, for that matter.

However, for most of us the problem isn't *whether* we

should verbalize our faith; rather, it's the *what* and *how* of it that concerns us. In the chapter on "Breaking Down Barriers" we worked on the *what*. Now, let's explore some simple suggestions about the *how*.

For most of us, verbalizing our faith has been a rather difficult task. Yet, it isn't difficult to talk about many other things. For example, I can very comfortably and easily engage a complete stranger in conversation about football or politics. The reason why is easy. I can do so, first of all, because I am personally interested in those things, and, secondly, because most of the men I meet are interested in those things too.

When you think of it, there are probably quite a few things you would feel comfortable talking about to a relative stranger. The weather, for instance. Or your family. Or your prospective husband or wife. In fact, it would be surprising if some of these things did not come up in a brief conversation with a stranger.

But when it comes to talking about our faith—well, that's another matter. You see, *that* could be offensive! But couldn't football or politics also be offensive? Suppose you start tearing down the other guy's team or his political party! The reason why it's not offensive is because, at least initially, you speak pretty generally and cautiously. You try to feel out the other person: whether he understands anything about football; whether he's interested; which teams he likes; etc. You start off simply, introduce the subject with a question or two, and proceed from there. Well, couldn't some of the same principles for establishing a conversation on sports or politics be used in introducing the subject of religious faith? At any rate, here are some pointers which I have found helpful.

Too Much, Too Rich, Too Foolish

To begin with, keep the conversation simple. This is

important even when a non-Christian shows obvious interest in the message you have to share. It is enough, in the beginning, to simply share about what Jesus Christ has done in your life and what He wants to do in the lives of all who will come to Him. It is enough to say that God has stepped into history in Jesus Christ in order to recycle our lives and make us whole again. Include the essential facts by all means, but be careful not to make it more difficult than it needs to be or ought to be. Dr. George Peters, one of my professors when I was in seminary, put it well. "Usually," he said, "we try to share too much, too rich, too fast."

To that, I would add still another category—"too foolish." Many of the methods that are suggested for getting a conversation started about Christ are merely gimmicks, and a few are utterly ludicrous. One, I'm told, suggests that the next time a smoker asks if you've got a match, you respond, "Not since the explosion!" When they ask what explosion, you say, "the explosion that took place in my life when I became a Christian!" I suspect that whoever proposed this introduction did so, tongue-in-cheek. But what a tragedy it is that there are also personal evangelism plans that *seriously* suggest such foolish approaches.

Start With a Question

Personally, I feel that one of the best ways to overcome our witnessing inhibitions is to work, not so much on "easy lessons in conversation" as on building relationships. When there is a relationship of trust between two persons, conversation can turn to almost any topic and be carried on sincerely and naturally.

But I also recognize there isn't always the time or opportunity to develop such a relationship, and we all encounter such situations. What do we do then?

I suggest starting with a question. You will, no doubt, notice that almost every witnessing plan does, and I think there are good reasons why. First of all, it's the most natural way to begin; and secondly, it's biblical. Jesus often began conversations about faith with a question. So did the apostles.

There is an interesting illustration of this in the Book of Acts in the story of Philip's encounter with the Ethiopian Eunuch. The Ethiopian, you will recall, was on his way home from Jerusalem, and he was sitting by his chariot, reading from the prophet Isaiah. Philip heard him reading and asked, "Do you understand what you're reading?"

"How can I?" said the Eunuch, "unless someone explains it to me."

So Philip went through the door his question had opened up, and the resulting conversation ended with the Ethiopian being baptized. Philip recognized, as so many have, that an excellent way to begin a conversation about spiritual matters is with an appropriate, natural, well-timed question.

However, two warnings are in order. First, if entrapment is taboo for law enforcement officers, it is even more out of order in the task of faith-sharing. Some series of questions are designed to do more than open up a conversation. They are intended to corner persons. Usually, such questions have only two possible answers, and no matter which one the prospect gives, you are ready with the perfect squelch. Then, that question, in turn, leads to another and another, and each time you are ready with your torpedos until presumably the victim is finally sunk.

Secondly, fixed questions do not meet the demands of the changing settings and circumstances of witnessing. Nor do they take into account the differences in the personalities and needs of the persons with whom you hope to share your faith. Nor do they encourage you to be as sensitive to the leading of the Holy Spirit as you need to be.

So to start with a question is a simple and worthwhile device for opening the door to meaningful spiritual conversation, but the questions must never be manipulative or canned.

The Art of Introduction

A second, and related, suggestion is to move away from pre-fab introductions (which are too mechanical and, therefore, unnatural) to the art of introduction (introducing your prospects to your Friend). Most of the popular methods of faith-sharing outline a plan of salvation. They are usually carefully and soundly devised introductions to the basics of the Christian faith. By and large they are worthwhile, and it is probably beneficial to memorize or at least to be familiar with one such plan. But when it comes to the actual task of faith-sharing, it is, in my opinion, best to forget such a step-by-step approach. Such introductions are helpful, but there are decided problems. It is far better to move from plans to a Person, from schemes to a Savior, from canned introductions to introducing a Friend.

When you do so, you have the decided advantage of speaking from experience, not hearsay. You are telling your prospect about what the Lord has done for *you*. That is what Jesus told the Gadarene demoniac to do, to go back to his home in the region of the Decapolis and to tell how the Lord had had mercy on him (Mark 5:19). Apparently, the man's testimony had its effect, because when, later on, Jesus went to that region, the crowds were with Him almost immediately (Mark 7:31f.).

Likewise, one of the things that makes the First Letter of John so powerful is John's statement of his own personal encounter with Christ: "That . . . which we have heard, which we have seen with our eyes, which we have looked at and our hands have touched—this we proclaim concerning the Word of life. The life appeared; we have seen it and testify to it, and we proclaim to you the eternal life, which was with the Father and has appeared to us. We proclaim to you what we have seen and heard . . ." (1 John 1:1-3). There is tremendous authority in a statement like that!

Dialogue, Not Monologue

Another suggestion for turning a conversation to matters of faith is to use the conversation itself. For example, I was recently in conversation with a man I did not know at all (we just happened to be sitting next to one another at the counter of a doughnut shop), and we were talking about the weather.

"Weather like this always makes me feel lousy," he said. "I always have lousy days when it's raining like this."

"You know, I can't think of the last time I had a really lousy day," I said. "Oh, I get discouraged occasionally; things don't go quite the way I'd like them sometimes; but I can't remember the last time something spoiled my whole day."

"Really?" he said. "How do you account for that?"

And that, you see, was my opportunity to, in a very natural way, share how enriching and exhilerating it is to know Christ as Lord of my life.

There's a danger at that point, however. You have to be careful that your conversation does not turn into a monologue. If what you've been able to share of your faith at that point turns into a sermon, its effect will most likely be zero. But if you're able to continue sharing it in an unthreatening way, if you share in such a way that he feels free to dialogue with you about it, then you have used your opportunity aright. Be sure, however, that you give him the freedom to change the course of the conversation if he chooses. If he does pick up on what you've said about your relationship with Jesus, try your best to affirm any remarks he makes that are consistent with what you are trying to convey. Give him credit for the insights he comes up with. Do everything you can to make him feel he is making a contribution to the conversation, and *he will be* if you are responding sensitively to his comments. Then, if the conversation progresses to the point where he becomes convinced of the truth of what you've been sharing, be sure to give him the credit for any decision he may make under the prompting of the Holy Spirit. Don't ever—not then, nor subsequently—claim any credit for his turning to the truth of the gospel.

Avoid "Religious" Language

Every vocation, every region, every generation has its own vocabulary. Ask an electronics technician about his work, and you will immediately be bombarded with terms like ohms, frequency modulation, impedence mismatch and the like, none of which will probably mean a thing to you, unless, of course, that happens to be your line of work too.

Go to a northern New England restaurant and ask for a hoagie (if you are from Pennsylvania) or a submarine (if you are from southern New England), and you will discover that it is really a grinder you're after.

In my grandfather's day, when you called something "square," that meant that it had four right angles and four equal sides; in my father's day, it meant "fair," "just," "honest," as in FDR's "Square Deal;" but when I was growing up, something square was something dull, trite, old-fashioned.

So what you do, where you live, and when you live all have a profound impact upon how you say what you say.

Each factor makes its own peculiar contribution to your vocabulary.

The Christian faith does that too. Christianity has its own impact upon what you say, and even the various branches of Christian thought influence it. Among evangelicals, for example, terms like "born again," "blood of the Lamb," "second coming," "beloved" and the like are all terms that are frequently used and well understood. And there is, of course, nothing at all wrong with the use of such terms, unless they are used with non-Christians who have no idea what they mean.

Suppose you were to visit a naval vessel for the first time, and as you board you tell the sailor who greets you on the quarter deck that you have an appointment with the captain. So he tells you to go to the 01 level, walk through the mess, turn right at the head, left at the wardroom, and climb the ladder to the bridge, where the captain will be waiting. For him to give such instructions to a civilian would be entirely inappropriate.

So it is for Christians. To use in-house evangelical language with the uninitiated is just as inappropriate. As the apostle Paul might put it, "I would rather speak five intelligible words to instruct others than ten thousand words in evangelicalese" (comp. 1 Cor. 14:19).

It is not enough, however, merely to *avoid* confusing terminology. You need to go the extra mile whenever you can. You need to translate what you are saying into language that stands the very best chance of being understood by the person with whom you are sharing. Just as Bible translators help us to understand certain obscure terms used in the New Testament, so we need to help others understand the concepts we seek to convey. For example, just as translators help us to understand what Mark means when he speaks of Jesus as "intestining" *(splanchnizomai)* on the crowds ("had compassion on them"), we need to clarify even statements like "when I was saved," for persons not familiar with the vocabulary of faith.

A Final Word

As I suggested earlier, I have the feeling that the most significant reason why we have difficulty talking about our faith is the fear of rejection. Actually, it occurs far less frequently than we fear it will, but rejection does happen, and we are afraid of it. Nobody wants to be the subject of ridicule. Nobody wants to be humiliated. There is a sense in which that is more difficult to face than outright persecution. But let me conclude with these two consoling words.

First, if you take seriously the suggestions made in this chapter, you will find that usually persons will be much more open to listening to what you have to share concerning the Good News.

Secondly, if you sincerely seek strength for witnessing boldly, God will grant it to you. He has made available His Holy Spirit for precisely that purpose, and you will not be the first to require it. As a matter of fact, Jesus forbade the disciples to carry out the Great Commission until they had been empowered by the Spirit (Luke 24:49). And Paul expressly asked the Christians at Ephesus, "Pray . . . for me, that whenever I open my mouth, words may be given me so that I will *fearlessly* make known the mystery of the gospel, for which I am an ambassador in chains. Pray that I may declare it *fearlessly*, as I should" (Eph. 6:19-20). The difference between compulsion and compassion as the motivation for witness is that simple. We need to use a little common sense; but it is the power of God working through us that makes the ultimate difference.

Chapter 10

Making the Most of Opportunities

Soon after I became a Christian, I joined a Bible study group which met regularly in the electronics shack on our ship. I was a young sailor stationed aboard the U.S.S. San Pablo, a small research vessel whose crew numbered only about 120.

To join a Bible study group on a ship that size was to make one's faith very public. Not only was I having opportunity to talk about my new-found faith in the group, but some of my non-Christian friends were giving me further opportunity by asking about my reasons for joining the group, and by asking what went on in the group's meetings.

By the time I was transferred to the Brooklyn Naval Base, where I spent two weeks waiting for my discharge date to arrive, I thought I had become quite proficient in sharing what good things the Lord had done for me (Mark 5:19). I also felt very free to share my faith when opportunities came along. But now the opportunities were not as frequent. And now when they did come, I found that the questions were tougher and the attitudes less open than they had been on the San Pablo.

The reason why I encountered more tough questions and closed minds, of course, was that instead of two years to build up relationships, I only had two weeks. And instead of 120 men, there were thousands. The situation was entirely different.

This reinforces what we have said about the need for building friendships and the kind of mutual trust that allows real freedom and openness in discussions about the faith. To me, it illustrates that the best evangelism is, indeed, friendship evangelism.

Paul Tokunaga wrote about a very important date that was to culminate with a very important question. The plans were carefully worked out and included a nostalgic drive, the perfect dinner out, low lights, mood music, and finally the question. However, everything went wrong. Not one facet of the carefully programmed evening went according to plan—except that the question got asked.

The answer floored him. It was yes! Then she explained, "I said yes, not because of tonight but because of the last year with you. For all the times you gave me . . . yourself—your time, your love, your overwhelming concern, your desire to see me become a better . . . me."[1]

The best evangelism is like that. It happens in a relationship of trust. As someone has said, "Your greatest witness is your deepest relationship." Therefore, our best opportunities for faith-sharing are made. They are made through commitment to individuals the Lord has asked us to befriend.

Many Christians ask, "Where can I find opportunities for witness?" But the better question may be, "How can I make opportunities for witness?" And the answer is by cultivating relationships.

Recognizing Opportunities

Does that mean we are to forget about the one-time meetings we have with persons, the casual acquaintances, or becoming involved in a door-to-door visitation program? By no means! There will be many special oppor-

tunities for witness that come along, and you will want to
be ready for them when they do. As I discovered at the
Brooklyn Naval Base, that the questions are tougher and
the attitudes less open at times, but that does not mean
you cannot witness effectively in such situations. And
more often than you might imagine, the Lord will send
persons to you who will not only give you a hearing, but
who are actually anxious for what you have to say.

When I was in college, I worked summers as an or-
derly. One day a nurse stopped me in the corridor and
said, "There's a lady who would like to see you in Room
220." I went to the room and introduced myself.

"Yes," she said, "one of the nurses told me that you are
a Christian."

"Yes," I said, "I am."

"Well, someone gave me this book," she said, "and I
just have to know more." She held up a book by a well-
known Christian author.

We had a good time of sharing, and the next morning I
returned to the young woman's room to share more of
what I knew about Christ. But the bed was empty. She
had died during the night on the operating table. How
glad I was that I had not put off taking advantage of the
opportunity the Lord had sent along!

A couple of years ago, I had an opportunity to share on
personal evangelism with some young people in a retreat
setting in southern Alabama. On my way home, on a flight
between Atlanta and Roanoke, Virginia, I worked on
translating some passages from my Hebrew Old Testament. I was seated next to the window, and to my left was
an attorney and his wife.

"Is that Greek?" he asked me. "I had some Greek back
in my undergraduate days."

"Actually, it's Hebrew," I said. "This is an Old Testament."

"Well, my undergraduate days were a long time ago," he said. "Are you Jewish? I'm Presbyterian myself."

"I'm a Mennonite," I said.

At this point the man's wife, who had known some Mennonites once, got into the conversation. She asked a number of questions, until her husband felt the urge to interrupt.

"Tell me," he said, "do you folks proselyte?"

I was horrified, but then he made some remarks which helped me to understand that by proselyte, he really meant evangelize.

"Sure we proselyte!" I said.

By now I had become convinced that neither this man nor his wife had a deep personal faith in Christ. They identified with a denomination and attended church occasionally. But that seemed to be about as far as it went. I asked the Lord to allow me to share more of the gospel with them. "Lord, give me the opportunity," I prayed. And then it came!

"*Why* do you proselyte?" he asked. There was not a hint of criticism in his question. He was genuinely interested. I was only too happy to answer!

If you are alert, you will find that God gives such opportunities often. Sometimes a complete stranger will ask you a question flat out which gives you a chance to share Christ. Sometimes His Spirit will guide you in turning a conversation into an occasion for witness. Sometimes a friend will refer you to someone who has a need. Your duty is to recognize such opportunities when they come and to take advantage of them.

Paul knew how to do that, and it was one of the keys to his effectiveness as an evangelist. In 1 Corinthians 16:9, he says, "I will stay on at Ephesus until Pentecost, because a great door for effective work has opened to me." On another occasion, "Paul had a vision of a man of

Macedonia standing and begging him, 'Come over to
Macedonia and help us.'" Luke adds, "After Paul had
seen the vision, we got ready at once to leave for
Macedonia, concluding that God had called us to preach
the gospel to them" (Acts 16:9-10).

Listening to the Spirit

One time, however, even though God had provided an
opportunity for witness, Paul did not feel comfortable in
staying long. He described the situation to the Corinthians like this: "Now when I went to Troas to preach the
gospel of Christ and found that the Lord had opened a
door for me, I still had no peace of mind, because I did not
find my brother Titus there. So I said good-by and went
on to Macedonia" (2 Cor. 2:12-13). For me, Paul's dilemma speaks to a problem which is both more difficult
and more common than that of recognizing opportunity—the problem of deciding priorities. Often our
situation is not one of having to find open doors, but of
having to determine when to go through!

However, the solution is simpler than we might think,
and in the next verses Paul indicates what it is. He says,
"But thanks be to God, *who always leads us. . . ."* When
we are sensitive to the leading of the Spirit, we will never
go wrong.

Paul did not go wrong. The Spirit would not give him
peace in staying on at Troas in spite of the open door
there. So he went to Macedonia in search of Titus. There
was trouble in the Corinthian church, and Titus had gone
there (probably bearing the letter which Paul says he had
written with many tears) to see if he could help resolve the
difficulties. Paul knew that the situation in Corinth was
serious enough to threaten the well-being of the whole
apostolic church if it wasn't settled. So he needed to move
on and find Titus.

There were two possible routes to Macedonia, one by sea and one over land. If Titus was on his way to Troas, Paul could easily have missed him by selecting the wrong route. But here, too, Paul sensed the Spirit's leading aright, and when he arrived at his destination, Titus was there.

Did Paul miss his opportunity in Troas? Indications are that he did not, and that the door was still wide open when he returned there in the spring.

If evangelism is a primary ministry of the Spirit in the world, if it is through the Spirit that God calls men and women to Christ, then it is obvious that we should look to Him, when in His service we are engaged in the task of sharing the Good News. We are His instruments and stewards of His gifts. When we fail to be obedient to His guidance in our evangelistic efforts, the harvest is bound to be pitiable. Indeed, any harvest there is will be there in spite of us and not in any way because of us! It will be a meager harvest, because the very best opportunities will have been missed.

The Primacy of Prayer

For Paul, opportunities were not just lucky breaks that you happened upon. They were God given. That meant that they were something to pray about. When Paul was instructing the Colossian Christians in the necessity of prayer, he asked them specifically to pray for opportunities for the spreading of the gospel. "Devote yourselves to prayer," he said, "being watchful and thankful. And pray for us too, that God may open a door for our message, so that we may proclaim the mystery of Christ, for which I am in chains" (Col. 4:2-3). Thus, just as it is impossible to think of evangelism without the Spirit (Acts 1:8), so it is impossible to think of evangelism without prayer.

Don't pray in general, however; *pray specifically*, for specific people. And *pray expectantly*. Jesus said, "I will do whatever you ask in my name, so that the Son may bring glory to the Father. You may ask me for anything in my name, and I will do it" (John 14:13-14).

I heard Doug Coe speak about the Christians in government who had been praying for Charles Colson's conversion. There were many of them. But most of them never dreamed that their prayers for Colson would be answered. Some of them would not even believe it when they heard it!

In Acts 12, there is a story about a prayer meeting that was going on at John Mark's mother's house. They were praying specifically that Peter, who was in prison, might be delivered. In response to their prayers, the Lord sent an angel and Peter was freed just as they had requested. But when there came a knock at the door, and Rhoda, the maid, came excitedly back upstairs announcing that it was Peter (She was so excited she had forgotten even to open the door!), they refused to believe her! "You're crazy!" they said. Then, deciding that that remark was a bit extreme, they rationalized, "Well, perhaps it was his angel!" But it was Peter's deliverance, not his angel's that they had been praying for!

So, like Paul, we need to pray for opportunities to share the gospel, and we need to pray for specific persons the Lord brings to our minds. Then, we need to ready ourselves for the opportunities He's going to bring us.

Very often, however, the Lord does not bring us opportunities but, rather, instructs us on how to create opportunities. Usually that involves cultivating relationships.

I cannot emphasize enough that most persons become disciples through the testimony and encouragement of someone they trust. When God's moment comes to convince a person of his need to repent and turn the reins of his life over to Christ, He usually speaks through a caring friend. In the context of the local congregation, that may mean a parent, a pastor, a Sunday school teacher, or, perhaps, a member of a Bible class or small group; but outside a local congregation, through whom does the Lord choose to speak? Well, again, it is usually through someone who has cared enough to establish and maintain a relationship.

Thus God's answer to our prayer for witnessing opportunities may be His challenge to us to take specific steps to befriend certain persons He has brought to our minds or has given us occasion to meet.

Establishing Relationships

The first step in doing that is simply to learn to listen (and to listen to learn). By careful listening you can discover such important information as a person's interests, his goals, his most important concerns, his most pressing needs, etc. It is amazing how much you can learn about a person with just a little careful listening. So begin by remembering that each person is a unique creation (there is no one else just like him) and that each person, in addition, has a unique background. Then, try to put yourself in that person's shoes. Try to understand who he is, where he's coming from, why he responds to certain situations in the way he does, etc. Then listen to learn what his desires, ambitions, aims, fears, burdens, needs, and the like are, so that you can be aware of situations you can plug into with a helping hand.

The second step is to show your interest in your prospective friend. There are a thousand ways to do it. Perhaps, for example, you have a neighbor who is struggling with depression, and you remember very vividly your own such struggles and how you overcame them. It will probably not be difficult for you to find a natural opportunity to share your experience. Or perhaps you have a friend at the shop who shares your interest in restoring old cars. Obviously, you have there a unique opportunity to establish a friendship. Or perhaps you may have a classmate who's lonely, or a niece who's doing a lot of soul-searching, or a neighbor family that enjoys backyard barbeques as much as your family. There are literally countless ways for you to show others that you'd like to be their friend.

The third step is to cultivate the friendship. This, of course, takes time, but the possibility of eventually introducing your new friend(s) to Christ, your best Friend, is well worth the patience you exercise. Friendships are cultivated in basically one way: by a continual demonstration that you really do care. That you show through the gift of your time, your attention, your trust, your loyalty—in other words, through the gift of yourself. You need to continue to spend time and effort on the man or woman or family God has given you, whoever it is you are seeking to befriend.

The fourth step is to share your faith. A vital part of your life is your faith in God. Eventually your friend will expect you to be open and free about that part of your life too. There may be small ways in which you can share it almost from the beginning, but there will come a time when you can share your testimony naturally and completely without it being a threat. That opportunity, of course, will have been part of your goal from the beginning. There are no secrets between truly good friends, and that includes secret friendships. Inevitably and *naturally* your relationship with Jesus *will* be shared! When your friend begins to respond to your friendship at a personal level, you will automatically begin to be alert to opportunities to share the Good News of the God who came among us in Christ.

These opportunities may come in the form of questions that are put directly to you concerning your faith. Or, for example, you may discover that your friend is open to visiting your Bible study group or a Christian concert. Or he may be interested in a book such as *Born Again.* If you invite your friend to a special occasion, you will certainly want to provide opportunity for him to reflect on the event. Often such an opportunity can be created by inviting your friend to dinner afterwards, or by inviting him out for coffee. It *is* important to get feedback *somehow* though, because your friend may have vital questions that need answering, or he may need assurance that you are not using the occasion just for the purpose of manipulating him, or he may be ready to make a positive response to what he has heard or seen. Dialogue will be important in any event however, and you will not want to miss a chance for it to happen.

Once dialogue on matters of faith begins, repeated encounters are almost certain to follow. This is especially true if your friend senses that you are relating to him in just that way—as a friend—and are not trying to trap him. It's essential to recognize this, because the opportunity for you to move beyond conversational testimony to your own experience to genuine discussion about Christ marks an important step forward in your relationship, and it would be sad were you to nullify it by insensitivity or wrong motives. This is an especially crucial time, and it is often just at this point that the Holy Spirit really begins to work in the life of the person you are seeking to make a disciple.

However, even if your friend does not respond to Christ, you should not give up or be discouraged. The time may not be ripe, and God may be waiting for some crisis event or special occasion that is coming to convict him. Or, it may be that it will be through someone else that his decision to follow Christ is finally made. God may simply be using you to plant the seed of the Word. He may use you to water that seed, and again, He may not; nevertheless, it is He and He alone who gives the increase.

So continue your expression of friendship, no matter what the results may appear to be. Let your friend know that your love and concern is not dependent upon his response but is free and unconditional, even as God's love in Christ is free and unconditional. In this way, you continue to give yourself opportunity, and not only yourself, but your unsaved friend as well.

Chapter 11

Life Together

D. T. Niles said that the purpose of evangelism is the recovery of wholeness. If that is true, then the task of caring evangelism is twofold. First, as we have already seen, it must lead the lost back to God. There is no wholeness apart from God. That is simply the way we are made. There is a God-shaped vacuum in each of us, and until it is filled there is an emptiness, a missing ingredient in life, an inner dissatisfaction that only He can take care of. Secondly, caring evangelism must lead the lost to God's people, for community is a vital part of wholeness too. The fact that God made Eve for Adam is his lasting comment on the necessity of a shared life.

Over three hundred years ago Francis Bacon wrote about the gracious and courteous man whose "heart is no island cut off from other lands, but a continent that joins to them." No doubt he felt those words deeply as he penned them, for he himself was a man "cut off." Convicted of bribery after a long and illustrious career, imprisoned for a time, and deprived of political office for the remainder of his life, he knew only too well the meaning of loneliness.

His contemporary, John Donne, who also knew the loneliness of a prison cell, used almost the same words but gave them a more provocative and memorable slant. He learned in a sickbed that "no man is an island," as he put it, and he shared the conviction he learned there that all of us are bound up with one another, not living our own independent existences, but sharing life together.

This truth is crucial to evangelism. There can be no wholeness apart from Christian community. As Donne put it, when someone is baptized into the church, it affects us all, for he "is thereby connected to that head (Christ) which is my head too, and ingrafted into that body whereof I am a member." And when someone dies it affects all of us. The bells toll not only for him, Donne said, but for us too.

The Wages of Sin

The trouble is that most men and women *do* perceive of themselves as islands. They do not have a conception of the shared life. Nor do they have that common connection in Christ that Donne spoke of.

That condition is directly related to sin. Sin, above all else, brings alienation. That is the essence of sin. The reason why Adam and Eve partook of the forbidden fruit was that they might have independence from God by having knowledge equal to His. The serpent sowed the seeds of mistrust, and suddenly the man and the woman felt the need for a balance of power. God was keeping something good from them, they thought. How could He, then, be on *their* side? What other reason could He have for instituting such a commandment? Why else would He forbid them to eat the fruit? It is the serpent who speaks the truth, not God! they thought. God has been merely trying to keep us under His thumb!

So Adam and Eve cast their vote in favor of independence, and they got it! They thought they wouldn't need God, that they could get along just fine on their own, but the result of turning their backs on God was far more tragic for them and their descendants than they ever imagined.

Adam and Eve opted for indepenence, and most of their descendants have opted for independence. For example, God fought the battles for the Children of Israel—drowned the Egyptians in the Red Sea; tumbled the walls of Jericho; frightened and defeated their enemies—until they opted for a king and independence. Then they had to fight their own battles.

But it wasn't just them, it is us too. That is why, as Richard Halverson has pointed out, even today "rift" describes society better than any other word. Not only have we turned our backs on God, we have turned our backs on each other. So there is rift between nations, races, the educated and illiterate, rich and poor, and on and on.

God honors our choice, though He has provided a better way. He allows us the illusion of independence and its accompanying rift if that is what we want. He even allows the ultimate rift to occur, though it grieves Him deeper than anything else—the eternal separation of death.

The Great Reversal

Paul says that Jesus came to reverse all that, however. He came to restore access to God and to one another. "Something there is that doesn't love a wall," wrote Robert Frost, and Paul's testimony is that God doesn't love a wall. He "has destroyed the barrier, the dividing wall of hostility," Paul writes, and "consequently, you are no longer foreigners and aliens, but fellow citizens with God's people and members of God's household" (Eph. 2:14,19). In other places as well, Paul seeks to justify his ministry to the Gentiles by pointing out that God has, in Christ, brought mankind together, so that there is no male nor female, freedman nor slave, etc. Some recent writers point out that that is the way we ought to view what Paul says in Romans 9-11—not as a parenthesis at all, but the heart of what he wanted to say.

The Joy of Fellowship

If the purpose of salvation is to reverse the alienating consequences of sin, then an evangelism that does not bring persons into community is not worthy of the name. Just as fellowship was an essential part of the life of the early church, so it must be today.

Fellowship with other Christians is a source of joy and strength that has no comparison. We may outwardly seek a life of independence from others, but inwardly there is a deep longing for and need for company. That longing may not be identified, but it is there just the same. Our failure to isolate our need does not diminish it. And when the need is finally met, the resulting joy is proof positive of the emptiness that really was. No wonder the aged apostle John wrote: "We proclaim to you the eternal life, which was with the Father and has appeared to us. We proclaim to you what we have seen and heard, so that you also may have fellowship with us. And our fellowship is with the Father and with his Son, Jesus Christ. We write this to make our [or your] joy complete" (1 John 1:3,4).

In his second letter, John again connects fellowship and joy. He says, "I have much to write to you, but I do not want to use paper and ink. Instead, I hope to visit you and talk with you face to face, so that our joy may be complete" (2 John 12). There is something about being with other Christians, something about their physical presence that brings a wholeness, a peace, a strength, a joy without which we would soon be wandering down the wayward paths again.

The Need For Fellowship

In his little book, *Life Together*, Dietrich Bonhoeffer wrote, "The believer feels no shame, as though he were still living too much in the flesh, when he yearns for the physical presence of other Christians. Man was created a body, the Son of God appeared on earth in a body, he was raised in the body, in the sacrament the believer receives the Lord Christ in the body, and the resurrection of the dead will bring about the perfected fellowship of God's spiritual-physical creatures."[1] It is inescapable, is it not? Man was made for man and can never be complete without him, his physical presence, his companionship.

Thomas Carlyle told about a widow who sought help from her neighbors, but they ignored her appeal. She is none of our concern, they thought. We have our own to look after. Sometime later, however, the widow came down with typhus and died. But not before she had infected those same neighbors who had refused assistance to her. Carlyle commented: "She proved her sisterhood. Her typhus fever killed them. They were brothers even though they denied it."

G. K. Chesterton found a friend and said to himself, "Dear me, he was made for me." Later, when he had found many more friends who seemed to have been made for him, he asked rhetorically, "Is it possible we were all made for each other all over the world?"

The Neglect of Fellowship

How sad it is that the modern church has so easily forgotten that.

David Augsburger, in *Communicating Good News*, compares the early church and the modern church. First he cites Acts 2:44-47, which says, "All the believers were together and had everything in common. Selling their possessions and goods, they gave to anyone as he had need. Every day they continued to meet together in the temple courts. They broke bread in their homes and ate together with glad and sincere hearts, praising God and enjoying the favor of all people. And the Lord added to their number daily those who were being saved." Then Augsburger cites what he calls "Facts 19:71-72," which comments on today's parallel:

> Every individual
> Each with his own opinions.
> Competing for his own possessions
> Looks out for his own.
> Assuming there are no needs.
> And once a week
> Going to their private church
> (With an annual communion)
> Each return to his castle,
> Fellowshipping with his family
> Over good "native" cooking
> After a short silent "grace,"
> And glad to be away from everybody.
> Occasionally there are
> New faces at church.
> And last year,
> Someone was saved.[2]

In 1 Corinthians 12, Paul describes the church as a body. Just as the body has many parts, so has the church. But they are all one. There are many parts but only one body, and there are many members but only one church. Because the parts of the body are one, they cannot function independently, and none can be called complete apart from the body. With the church it is the same. Each member needs the others, and each one is less than the whole.

It is impossible to think of the Christian life apart from mutual interdependence. Christianity without community is like an ocean without water or a library without books. That is one of the things we symbolize in Christian baptism, when a new believer joins the church, for in the words of Paul, "By one Spirit we were all baptized into one body" (1 Cor. 12:13).

Not long ago a high school chorus visited our congregation and taught us to sing Avery and Marsh's endearing song that says that I am the church, you are the church, and we are the church together. We all stood as we sang it through several times, and each time we embraced someone standing close to us. Somehow, we must help the words of that song to become a reality in the experience of each new disciple in our churches, just as they were a reality for the believers whose story Luke recounts in Acts. Caring evangelists must see to it that new believers are incorporated into the life of the church.

Introduction to the Fellowship

How is that accomplished? How *do* you incorporate a new believer into the life of the church? Here are some of the possibilities:

1. Get your friend involved in a Sunday school class. A small one! Large lecture-type classes are fine for imparting knowledge, for inspiration, and for motivating men and women to service for Christ. But the new believer needs the personal element that a large class cannot adequately provide. More often than not, it is the depersonalization and anonymity he has experienced in contemporary society that set him looking for something better in the first place. He is tired of assembly-line approaches, tired of being a number, tired of bigness. To meet his needs, the church needs to be a place where he can become truly human. He needs a place where he can have opportunity to raise his questions, test his conclusions, and receive personal affirmation. The very fact that

God has won him through friendship and caring suggests his continuing need.

2. Involving him in a small group is even better. Small groups have varying emphasis, of course. Some emphasize mission, some emphasize sharing, and some devote themselves to Bible study. But invariably, there will be *koinonia*, fellowship. The small group was the basic unit of the church during the first two hundred years, and it is significant how often the word "fellowship" is connected with its meeting. Whenever there is vital fellowship, edification takes place, believers are equipped, and the church advances its witness. That was the case with the New Testament church, and it is true of today's as well.

3. Introduce your friend to members of the congregation who are most likely to offer the continuing support he needs. You cannot do it alone. If your friend is to mature, he will need additional person-to-person relationships, too.

Discipling

Perhaps the most significant benefit of the shared life is the mutual exhortation and encouragement that happens. Marlin Jeschke has called it "discipling," a term I have grown rather fond of. The reason for discipline is, as the Book of Hebrews puts it, "so that none of you may be hardened by sin's deceitfulness" (3:13). Furthermore, it states that this discipling is to take place daily!

Hebrews 10:25 has often been used as a proof-text validating the necessity of attending preaching services. But taken with the preceding verse, the real thrust becomes crystal clear: "And let us consider how we may spur one another on toward love and good deeds. Let us not give up meeting together, as some are in the habit of doing, but let us encourage one another—and all the more as you see the day approaching."

Few Christians fully realize the importance of this encouragement and admonition in the life of the church. But without it the church would very soon cease to exist. As Hubmaier said in the days of the Reformation, "Where there is no brotherly admonition, no church is to be found."

Matthew 18:15-18 and Galatians 6:1 are two classic texts which describe how discipling takes place. They are designed to instruct us on how to restore (not punish!) the brother or sister who has gone astray. The latter passage puts it this way: "Brothers, if a man is trapped in some sin, you who are spiritual should restore him gently." Perhaps this is what Proverbs calls "the faithful wounds of a friend."

The Importance of Discipling

Have we realized how important such faithful wounds really are? James wrote: "My brothers, if one of you should wander from the truth and someone should bring him back, remember this: Whoever turns a sinner away from his error will save him from death and cover many sins" (James 5:19-20).

What greater motivation could there be for the discipline of the shared life than that? Who can measure the preciousness of a soul? Men have stabbed at it, but if you want to know the real worth of a soul, look to God's estimate of it! God the omnipotent, who made the worlds and all that is in them, who sustains the universe—what is *His* estimate of it? When God estimates the value of a human soul, He doesn't think in terms of the vastness of His creation, nor does He consider the glories of heaven. Instead, He looks upon His risen Son and says, "He is the value of a precious soul!" And James says that whoever brings back a sinner from the error of his way saves his soul!

Conclusion

So, you see, the discipline of life together is an essential part of evangelism. It ensures that wholeness really comes to the new believer (and what else is the meaning of salvation?). And it helps to strengthen him or even restore him if he wanders astray.

Christianity without community, then, is meaningless. Evangelism itself is soon undermined if people discover that in the absence of the shared life, to belong or not to belong to a church really makes no difference, with life in the church just as artificial and depersonalized as in the plastic, computer culture around it.

Chapter 12

The Importance of Following Through

Follow-through is essential not only in swinging a golf club or baseball bat, but in whatever we do. Certainly it is vital to the task of personal evangelism. Often, however, Christian evangelists have been concerned only with getting "decisions." Some have gone further and talked about the need for follow-up, but there is a great deal of difference between following up and following through.

A Sunday school teacher asked her pupils, "Who loves everybody?" One eight-year-old replied, "My Dad does, 'cause he's running for office." That kind of love seldom survives the campaign season, but Christian love needs to be different. The caring evangelist keeps on caring for those who have come to Christ through him *for life!*

Research has shown that an alarming number of those who make public commitments in evangelistic campaigns soon drop out of the church or never become connected with a local congregation at all. The results are better when a campaign of "pre-evangelism" has preceded the actual crusade, but the reason why is because there is more likely to be adequate follow-through when, through "friendship evangelism" (It's called "Operation Andrew," for example, in the Graham campaigns), there are actual relationships being established before the evangelist comes, as opposed to mere contacts. This, again, illus-

trates the advantage of the style of evangelism we have
been espousing in this book, a style which cannot be
consistent without long-term commitments to the persons being discipled.

We discussed one of the elements in adequate follow-
through in the last chapter. If a young Christian is to grow
and mature in Christ, you will need to involve him in
fellowship of the body. But you also should personally
follow through with the one you have led to Christ.

Consistent Christian Living

One aspect of that task is to live as consistent a Christian
life as you can, seeking to continually grow in Christ
yourself. In New Testament times a rabbi's disciples
eventually graduated and became rabbis themselves.
That was not true, however, of Christ's disciples. Christ's
disciples *always* remain disciples. There is no such thing
as a "mature" Christian, only one who is maturing!

This is one of the most significant facets of following-
through, to be moving on in the walk with Christ. Then
you can say, as Paul said, "Follow my example, as I follow
the example of Christ" (1 Cor. 11:1). But chances are you
will not even need to say it; by your very walk you will
inspire your disciples to imitate you in following Christ.

That is not enough, however. You also need to assist the
new disciple in such things as developing a consistent
devotional life, learning to interpret the Word, and dis-
covering the joy of discipling others.

Paul's Follow-Through Program

Paul obviously recognized that, as illustrated by this
statement: "We proclaim him, counseling and teaching
everyone with all wisdom, so that we may present everyone perfect in Christ. To this end I labor, struggling with
all the energy he so powerfully works in me" (Col.

1:28,29). But how did Paul actually conduct his follow-through program? Well, in a number of ways:

First, he visited those for whom he felt accountable.

Acts 13 and 14 describes the ministry of Paul and Barnabas in Antioch, Iconium, Lystra, and Derbe. Luke says that after they had won a large number of disciples in Derbe however, "they returned to Lystra, Iconium and Antioch, strengthening the disciples and encouraging them to remain true to the faith. 'We must go through many hardships to enter the kingdom of God,' they said (clearly pointing out the cost of discipleship)." Then, Luke says, "Paul and Barnabas appointed elders for them in each church and, fasting, committed them to the Lord, in whom they had put their trust" (Acts 14:21-23). But that was not the end of the matter. In the next chapter we find Paul proposing to Barnabas once again, "Let us go back and visit the brothers in all the towns where we preached the word of the Lord and see how they are doing" (v. 36).

We need to maintain that kind of personal contact with those whom we disciple too. It may not always be possible, but whenever it is, the value of such fellowship must never be underestimated. Jesus remained in almost constant touch with His disciples. Even when He was ready to be received out of their midst, He promised them, "I will be with you always, to the very end of the age" (Matt. 28:20).

Secondly, Paul often designated someone to visit his disciples in his place.

We have already mentioned Titus' visit to Corinth in behalf of Paul. Another example is his sending of Timothy to the Thessalonians. It wasn't that Paul didn't want to go himself. Indeed, he says that he tried again and again to go, but each time Satan hindered him. "So when we could stand it no longer, we thought it best to be left by ourselves in Athens. We sent Timothy, who is our brother and God's fellow worker in spreading the gospel of Christ, to strengthen and encourage you in your faith. . . ." (1 Thess. 3:1,2).

Notice the heart of the man! Paul had a genuine love for the men and women in that city. He was not like Carlyle who said of London, "There are three and a half million people in this city—mostly fools!" No, Paul had the love of a father toward his children, and, in fact, on occasion he describes himself that way (e.g., 1 Cor. 4:14-15). When he was not able to follow through personally, as we sometimes cannot, he saw to it that a trusted friend did.

Pastors often get such requests. Frequently I receive letters asking me to follow through with some friend's young disciple. Recently I was at a meeting in Charlottesville, Virginia, and a pastor asked me, "Do you remember meeting Richard _____ last year?" I did, and the pastor told me that he would soon be coming to our community to attend college. "Will you be a brother to him?" he asked. What a privilege he was offering me!

Thirdly, Paul followed through by letter.

Just the other day I received a letter in the mail with a familiar return address. It was from my friend, Clarence Fretz. When I was still in the Navy, Clarence heard of my conversion and began writing to me. He has been kind of a spiritual father to me ever since. We do not get to visit often, and we do not write more than once or twice a year usually. But when a letter does come from Clarence, it is invariably opened first. I know that there is going to be real food for my soul in the letter, and I know that the questions, the concerns, and the encouragement that I will find in it represent the caring of a brother who loves the Master deeply and who loves me too.

I need not say very much about Paul's ministry of follow-through by letter. It is probably the best-known aspect of this part of his continuing care for his disciples. But have you ever thought about how most of the New Testament is follow-through literature, from Luke's Gospel to Jesus' letter to the churches? Today we have the additional means of telephones and cassette recordings. There really is no excuse for not following through, is there?

The Hazards of Discipleship

Not only is follow-through important for insuring the growth of a new Christian, it is also important in helping with certain difficulties that may come along.

First, there is the problem of doubt.

Fosdick used to lament the fact that the word *doubt* seemed to be irreversibly confined to the semantic doghouse of religion. He was right in lamenting it, but, fortunately, attitudes have changed. Most Christians need to wrestle with doubts from time to time, especially new Christians, and today we are generally ready to recognize that. There have been times when most of us could have prayed with the father of the boy with an evil spirit, "I do believe, [but] help me overcome my unbelief" (Matt. 9:24). There have been times when most of us could have asked with John the Baptist, "Are you the one who was to come, or should we expect someone else" (Matt. 11:3)? So just as an infant is continually in need of the assurance of his mother's presence, so the new disciple needs constant reassurances that he has been fully forgiven and accepted by God through Christ.

Then, there is the problem of peer pressure.

Very often, when men and women give Christ His rightful place and choose to be His disciples, they are harrassed and ridiculed by their friends and associates. That was one of the great fears of the Christian friends of Chuck Colson after he was converted. That is why they stuck so close to him and why we should stick close to those who are led to Christ through us. It is not enough to get your friend going to Sunday school or to a worship service. He is going to confront challenges to his faith that he will not have opportunity to discuss in those settings, and he is going to have questions of his own that grow out of such challenges. Therefore, it will be essential, especially in the first few months, for you to be available to your friend. And even if he does not make many efforts to come to you for answers and encouragement, you should be checking in with him and continuing to nurture your relationship.

There is also the problem of discouragement.

How does a new Christian respond to failure? What happens when all at once he becomes aware that he is slipping back into old habits? Often, he will become discouraged. Even men and women who have been Christians for many years sometimes have to face this. Both new and not-so-new Christians often set very high standards for themselves, and when they fail to meet them, they become disheartened and depressed. Without encouragement and support, that depression can become defeat. The Lord is always ready to strengthen such persons, but often that strength comes through the insights and help of Christian brothers and sisters.

Therefore, we need to be ready with the word of consolation, encouragement, exhortation, or other help. We need to remind our discouraged Christian friends, for example, that while we have God's Word so that we will not sin, nevertheless, if we do sin, "we have one who speaks to the Father in our defense," and "if we confess our sins, he is faithful and just and will forgive us our sins and purify us from all unrighteousness" (1 John 2:1; 1:9).

There are other hazards that are encountered by believers too, but I am merely interested in listing enough of them to further press the point of the need for follow-through. This important commitment is probably the most neglected aspect of disciple-making; yet, it is the most crucial one of all, if the fruit of our efforts is ever to mature.

Effectiveness

Three of the most important considerations for effective follow-through are commitment, consistency, and communication.

First, as we've already suggested, *we need to be committed to the task.* Authentic follow-through involves a heavy commitment of time and emotional energy. It necessitates a reordering of our priorities, and that is, perhaps, more difficult today than any time in the past. There are all sorts of things crying for our attention, and the choices we must make concerning them are not a matter of the good versus the bad, but the good versus the better. When it comes to discipling, however, we cannot afford to hedge. Half-hearted efforts at discipling may be worse than none. If we build a relationship with someone and lead him to Christ, we'd better be prepared to carry on with the task. Remember, the decision to follow Christ is only the convert's first step. It's just the beginning, both for him and for the one through whom the Lord has persuaded him to take that step.

Secondly, we need to be consistent in our lives. We've already mentioned this one too, but it cannot be emphasized enough. Discipleship is more caught than taught; it is more a transference of life than it is a disseminating of information. That means that our lives must be observable, which necessitates our availability to the new believer and, beyond that, means that something had better be happening in our lives—something called growth. So we need to give attention to the spiritual development of our new Christian friends, yes; but an essential part of that is giving attention to the spiritual development of ourselves!

Thirdly, *we need to be communicating the teachings of the New Testament.* Jesus said that we are to teach new disciples to obey all that He has commanded us. To do that, we have to be well-grounded in the Word ourselves. Reflect on what that means for you personally. Do you have regular times set aside for Bible study? Or do you depend only upon what you can assimilate on Sunday mornings? That can never be enough. Regular, systematic Bible study is vital to effective follow-through.

Along with that, it is not a bad idea to become familiar with some of the many good books and other tools that are available to disciplers. Most denominations and many independent organizations have excellent training programs available.

Still another way to insure that Christ's teachings get across is by getting the new disciple into a congregation where the Bible is taught. Reinforcement is a vital part of the learning process, and exposing new believers to settings such as Sunday school and corporate worship in which there is solid biblical teaching insures that such reinforcement takes place. Also, there are dynamics in teaching that comes across a pulpit or lectern that makes for a different, yet essential kind of impact, than those which come through your times of personal sharing.

Finally, communicating the teachings of Christ includes training new disciples to become disciplers themselves. There is only one way for the gospel to be effectively communicated throughout the whole world, and that is through the multiplication of disciplers.

It is possible, however! Suppose you win two friends to the Lord during the next six months, and each of them, in turn, wins two more during the next six months, and so on. Within a single generation the gospel could conceivably be communicated to every man and woman on the face of the earth! The first century Christians probably came closest to that goal, but there is no reason why twentiety century Christians can't see just as amazing results!

Thus, we need to do more than obey the Great Commission ourselves; we need to teach others to obey it too. This is the ultimate goal of follow-through, of course—to teach those new friends we've made for God how to lead others to Christ and follow through with them, themselves!

Chapter 13

Where She Stops Nobody Knows

As they spun the wheel of fortune, the old carnival barkers used to say, "Round and round she goes and where she stops nobody knows." There is a sense in which that is true of Christian witness, for we never know where the effects of a word for Christ will end. This can be illustrated by countless stories.

A Sermon, a Tract, and a Witness

A Christian worker in Nottingham, England called on a dying lady one time and found her rejoicing in Christ. "How did you get to know the Lord Jesus," he asked her. She thrust a piece of newspaper into his hand and said, "Read this." It was part of a sermon by Spurgeon that had been published in an American newspaper. The Christian worker asked the lady how she came by the newspaper, and she explained that she had received a parcel from Australia, and the paper had been used to wrap it! Imagine!—A sermon preached in London and published in an American newspaper had found its way to Australia and then back to Nottingham, England, where a woman found Christ as the result!

Long ago, a timid Christian woman handed Richard Baxter a leaflet, which led him to Christ, and he wrote a book called *Saints' Everlasting Rest*. Through that book, countless others came to know Christ, among them, Philip Doddridge, William Wilberforce, and Leigh Richmond, who in turn brought countless others to Christ. Even today we feel their influence. In the great hymn, "Hark the glad sound," for example, the voice of Doddridge still speaks mightily to our hearts. And who has not felt the repercussions, even these many generations later, of Wilberforce's powerful attacks on the tyranny of slavery? Perhaps more than any other individual, he gave the world a conscience about the cruelty and wrongness of selling fellow human beings.

There are many such chains of influence even in our own communities and among our own friends, if we will but reflect a few moments. For example, I know a young man who developed a relationship with two prisoners in a county jail. Eventually he was able to convince them of their need of Christ. On one of his visits to the jail a short while later, the jailor told the young man that he had just become a Christian. He explained that two of the prisoners—the same two with whom the young man had been sharing his faith—had led him to the Lord!

The Legacy of Edward Kimball

One of the most amazing examples of the pyramiding effects of faith sharing that I have come across, however, was told by James H. Semple in a 1967 article in *Christianity Today*, entitled, "Passing the Torch of Evangelism."[1] Most of us remember the story of Edward Kimball, who was D. L. Moody's Sunday school teacher, but we probably do not remember his name. When Moody was seventeen he had gone to Boston to look for work, which he found with his uncle, who owned a shoe store. His uncle encouraged him to attend church, and Edward Kimball became his Sunday school teacher. One day Kimball paid young Moody a visit at the store, and while the youth was putting away shoes in the back room, he convinced him to give his life to Christ. Kimball, who had become aware that he probably did not have long to live, also visited each of the other members of his class and led them to Christ as well.

Years later, when he was preaching in England, Moody, who became one of the great evangelists of all time, was telling the story of Kimball in the church of F. B. Meyer. One of the teachers in the church was so inspired by the story that she told it to her Sunday school class. As a result, each member gave her heart to Christ. This event in Meyer's church revolutionized his ministry.

But not only was Meyer's ministry revolutionized, so was another young minister's through Meyer's preaching. When he was preaching in the United States in Moody's school in Northfield, Massachusetts, he put the emphasis, as he so often did, on the need for consecration. "If you are not willing to give up everything for Christ," he said, "are you willing to be made willing?" That shook a young man sitting in the back row, and as a result, his entire ministry was transformed. The man's name was J. Wilbur Chapman. Chapman not only became a great evangelist in his own right, but he became one of the most influential churchmen of his time. He was a leader in the YMCA movement, the first director of the Winona Lake Bible Conference, and a moderator of the Presbyterian general assembly.

Meyer influenced many others as well, including the great Baptist preacher, Robert G. Lee, last of the orators in the William Jennings Bryan tradition. Lee was a distraught student at Furman University at the time, but a message by Meyer turned his life around.

But let's go back and trace the chain still further through Chapman.

When Chapman was associated with the YMCA, an

organization that Moody and he had effectively breathed new life into, he met a former professional baseball player, now a YMCA clerk. Later, Chapman turned over his ministry in evangelism to the man when he returned to the pastorate. The clerk, whose name was William Sunday, had worked intimately with Chapman in his crusades for two years. Now, through superb organizational skills and sensational preaching he was able to preach to more than a hundred million during his lifetime, an incredible feat! It is said that as many as a million "hit the trail" through his ministry.

In 1924, Billy Sunday, as he came to be known, preached in Charlotte, North Carolina, and through his preaching there, a layman's group was founded that sought to carry on a witness for Christ in the community. In 1932, they organized a crusade and called Mordecai Ham in to preach.

Ham's preaching was deeply disturbing to one 16-year-old high school senior who sat in the tent night after night. He and his friend, Grady Wilson, thought they could "escape" by sitting behind the preacher in the choir. But such was not to be. Finally, young Billy Graham and his friend Grady, like many others who attended those meetings over the three months Ham was there, went forward to indicate they were ready to begin their life with Christ.

Minor Events With Major Consequences

Someone has said that even the smallest moments in our relationships with others have impact for eternity. Undoubtedly that is right. And undoubtedly some of our seemingly least significant actions have unfathomable repercussions. You and I do not have to think long before we can recall small turns of events, minor incidents in our lives, that have already made major differences. They have greatly affected what is and what might have been. When viewed in terms of the lives of the many we touch and in terms of our influence upon the generations to come, it becomes unfathomable. Our signatures will be upon the lives of many more than we can ever imagine. Think of the effects of the sin of the first man and woman, for example. Think of the influence of Jesus and the handful of men who sat at His feet those three years or less.

Who knows, then, what you convey of Christ through that one relationship may mean? Who knows what that one brief testimony about the Lord Jesus may mean from the perspective of eternity? Who knows what may result from your posting *your* thesis on *your* Wittenburg door, or from your visit with a young man in the back room of a shoe store, or from your reading aloud the preface of Luther's commentary on Romans, as someone did on the night when Wesley's heart was "strangely warmed?" You never know!

In that light, what could be more important than the act of communicating the gospel to your friends? And what relationships could be more important than the ones that will give you the opportunity to do just that?

What Is Your Potential?

You have every bit as much potential for the kingdom as Edward Kimball had. Your smallest witness can have immense impact. Your deepest relationship is bound to! Jesus' disciples did not have much real ability from the world's standpoint. They were not educated, they were not trained in public speaking, they didn't have the right political or religious connections; yet the Bible says they turned the whole world upside down. But Christ wasn't looking for ability, you see. And His primary interest today isn't ability either. It is not your ability that matters;

it is your availability! God wants to use you to accomplish great things for His kingdom. He wants, especially, to work through you to win the lost back to Himself. Are you available? Are you willing to turn your life over to Him for His use? If you are not willing, are you willing to be made willing?

How We've Failed

How sad it is that many of those who have come to know the joys and blessings of a relationship with Christ, have had such great reluctance to share their Good News with others. Perhaps some of the unnatural methodologies that have been espoused have had something to do with that reluctance. Perhaps pastors have been too busy laying guilt trips on their congregations, rather than giving them real help. Perhaps we have oversubscribed to the clergy-layman dichotomy that regards ministers as "hired spokesmen for religion among men," as Peter Marshall used to describe it, or as "paid witnesses," as someone else dubbed it. But whatever the reasons, there is a crucial need in the world for witnesses, and it is sad to see the only ones who have the credentials to fill that role, neglecting the task that has been entrusted to them.

Sometimes when we think of the first-century Christians, we think of ourselves and say, "If only I could be the extraordinary sort of person many of them were." But they were extraordinary persons only because they allowed God to work through them. In every other respect, they were ordinary persons just like you and me. The difference was that they did not need to be instructed in witnessing methodology, like us. Neither did they need to be harrangued about the need for evangelizing. You search the New Testament in vain for such admonitions.

Barefoot Christians

Hugh Price Hughes was one of the great Methodist preachers of the nineteenth century. He was a man of unbounded zeal, especially when it came to missions. Part of the Hughes legacy is this poignant parable that asks the reason why faith-sharing is so difficult for us. It goes like this:

I arrived in that city early one morning. It was cold and there were flurries of snow on the ground. As I stepped from the train to the platform I noticed that the baggage-man and the redcap were warmly attired in heavy coats and gloves, but oddly enough, they wore no shoes. Repressing my impulse to ask the reason for this odd practice, I went into the station and inquired the way to the hotel. My curiosity, however, was increased by the discovery that no one in the station wore any shoes. Boarding the streetcar, I saw that my fellow travelers were likewise barefoot; and upon arriving at the hotel I found that the bellhop, clerk, and residents were all devoid of shoes.

Unable to restrain myself any longer, I asked the manager what the practice meant.

"What practice?" said he.

"Why," said I, pointing to his bare feet, "why don't you wear shoes in this town?"

"Ah," said he, "that is just it. Why don't we?"

"But what is the matter? Don't you believe in shoes?"

"Believe in shoes, my friend! I should say we do. That is the first article of our creed, shoes. They are indispensable to the well-being of humanity. Such frostbite, cuts, sores, and suffering as shoes prevent! It is wonderful!"

"Well, then, why don't you wear them?" I asked, bewildered.

"Ah," he mused, "that is just it. Why don't we?"

Though considerably nonplussed I checked in, secured

my room, and went directly to the coffee shop. There I deliberately sat down by an amiable-looking but barefoot gentleman. Friendly enough, he suggested, after we had eaten, that we look about the city.

The first thing we noticed upon emerging from the hotel was a huge brick structure of impressive proportions. He pointed to this with pride.

"You see that?" said he. "That is one of our outstanding shoe manufacturing establishments!"

"A *what?*" I asked in amazement. "You mean you make shoes there?"

"Well, not exactly," said he, a bit abashed. "We talk about making shoes there, and, believe me, we have one of the most brilliant young fellows you have ever heard. He talks most thrillingly and convincingly every week on this great subject of shoes. Just yesterday he moved the people profoundly with his exposition of the necessity of shoe-wearing. Many broke down and wept. It was really wonderful!"

"But why don't they wear them?" said I insistently.

"Ah, that is just it. Why don't we?"

Just then, as we turned down a side street, I saw through a cellar window a cobbler actually making a pair of shoes. Excusing myself from my friend, I burst into the little shop and asked the shoemaker how it happened that his shop was not overrun with customers. "Nobody wants my shoes," he said. "They just talk about them."

"Give me what pairs you have already," I said eagerly, and paid him thrice the amount he modestly asked. Hurriedly I returned to my friend and offered them to him, saying, "Here, my friend, one of these pairs will surely fit you. Take them, put them on. They will save you untold suffering."

"Ah, thank you," he said, with embarrassment, "but you don't understand. It just isn't being done. The front families, well, that is just it. Why don't we?"

And coming out of the city of Everywhere, over and over and over that question rang in my ears: "Why don't we? Why don't we? Why don't we?"

The Possibilities

The situation can be different, however. And had we a real conception of the potential, it might be! "When one life is changed," said Thomas L. Johns, "the world is changed." And he was right!

When Saul met the Lord on the Damascus Road and became a new man, Paul, the cities of Athens, Corinth, Rome, Ephesus, London, New York, Los Angeles, not to mention the suburbs and villages and hamlets of the world, had no idea of the influence he would have upon them.

When Peter and John and the other disciples became empowered by the Holy Spirit, it wasn't long before people said that they were turning the whole world upside down.

When, suddenly, the Lord got hold of Martin Luther through Paul's letter to the Romans, and showed him the importance of the doctrine of justification by faith, a Reformation was born.

When Edward Kimball, as we have seen, led his Sunday school pupil, Dwight L. Moody, to the Lord in the back room of a Boston shoe store, a chain of events was set in motion that affected the lives of F. B. Meyer, Wilbur Chapman, Billy Sunday, and Billy Graham, and not one of those men left the world like he found it.

That is why every opportunity to share the gospel is an opportunity not to be wasted. Every opportunity which has the potential for changing lives is an occasion we don't want to let pass if we can help it. With every opportunity comes the weight of responsibility, and knowing what the possibilities are—life changing possibilities, world-changing possibilities—we must be faithful. That must always and ever be the mindset of those who have been entrusted with the gospel, God's Good News people.

Notes

Chapter 3
1. The comparison between angling and net fishing is based in part on an article by John H. Yoder, "Jesus' Kind of Fisherman," in *Gospel Herald*, 1 May 1973, p. 375.

Chapter 4
1. This chapter is adapted from "Caring Evangelism," by Arthur G. McPhee in *Gospel Herald*, 20 August 1974, pp. 628-29.
2. Menno Simons, *Complete Writings of Menno Simons*, ed. John C. Wenger (Scottdale, Pa.: Herald Press, 1956), p. 92.

Chapter 7
1. Arthur G. McPhee, *The Mennonite Hour*, "Emmanuel, God With Us," No. 102, © 1977. Used by permission of Mennonite Broadcasts, Inc.

Chapter 10
1. "Friendship Evangelism," in *His*, student magazine of Inter-Varsity Christian Fellowship, December 1974, p. 31. © 1974. Used by permission.

Chapter 11
1. From *Life Together*, by Dietrich Bonhoeffer, trans. John W. Doberstein (New York: Harper & Row, 1954), pp. 19-20.
2. David W. Augsburger, *Communicating Good News* (Scottdale, Pa.: Herald Press, 1972), p. 86.

Chapter 13
1. "The Legacy of Edward Kimball" is adapted from "Passing the Torch of Evangelism," in *Christianity Today*, 27 October 1967, p. 15. © 1967. Used by permission.

Bibliography

The Message of Evangelism
1. Augsburger, Myron S. *Invitation to Discipleship.* Scottdale, Pa.: Herald Press, 1964.
2. Watson, David. *I Believe In Evangelism.* Grand Rapids: William B. Eerdmans Publishing Co., 1976.

Personal Evangelism
1. Augsburger, David. *Communicating Good News.* Scottdale, Pa.: Herald Press, 1972.
2. Bender, Urie. *The Witness.* Scottdale, Pa.: Herald Press, 1965.
3. Ford, Leighton. *Good News Is for Sharing.* Elgin, Ill.: David C. Cook Publishing Co., 1977.
4. Griffin, Em. *The Mind Changers.* Wheaton, Ill.: Tyndale House Publishers, Inc., 1976.
5. Hendricks, Howard G. *Say It With Love.* Wheaton, Ill.: Victor Books, 1972.
6. Little, Paul E. *How To Give Away Your Faith.* Downers Grove, Ill.: InterVarsity Press, 1962.

Following Through
1. Coleman, Robert E. *The Master Plan of Evangelism.* Old Tappan, N. J.: Fleming H. Revell, 1963.
2. Henrichsen, Walter A. *Disciples Are Made—Not Born.* Wheaton, Ill.: Victor Books, 1976.
3. Jeschke, Marlin. *Discipling The Brother.* Scottdale, Pa.: Herald Press, 1972.
4. Kuhne, Gary W. *The Dynamics of Personal Follow-up.* Grand Rapids: Zondervan Publishing House, 1976.
5. Wilson, Carl. *With Christ in the School of Disciple Building.* Grand Rapids: Zondervan Publishing House, 1976.

ZONDERVAN FACTORY OUTLET

BV 3790 .M27 1978
Friendship evangelism : the
caring way to share your
faith / Arthur G. McPhee